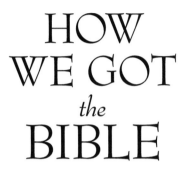

HOW
WE GOT
the
BIBLE

HOW WE GOT *the* BIBLE

THIRD EDITION
REVISED AND EXPANDED

Neil R. Lightfoot

Baker Books
A Division of Baker Book House Co
Grand Rapids, Michigan 49516

Published by Baker Books
a division of Baker Book House Company
P.O. Box 6287, Grand Rapids, MI 49516-6287

Fifth printing, May 2006

Printed in the United States of America

Library of Congress Cataloging-in-Publication Data
Lightfoot, Neil R.
     How we got the Bible / Neil R. Lightfoot.—3rd ed., rev. and expanded.
          p.   cm.
     Includes bibliographical references (p.) and index.
     ISBN 10: 0-8010-1252-X
     ISBN 978-0-8010-1252-5
     1. Bible—History. I. Title.
     BS445.L47 2003
     220'.09—dc21   2003003625

For Ollie

The real text of the sacred writers is competently exact; . . . nor is one article of faith or moral precept either perverted or lost . . . choose as awkwardly as you will, choose the worst by design, out of the whole lump of readings.

—Richard Bentley

I can only state my own conviction that a study of the history and condition of the Greek text solves far more difficulties than it creates.

—J. B. Lightfoot

It is reassuring at the end to find that the general result of all these discoveries and all this study is to strengthen the proof of the authenticity of the Scriptures, and our conviction that we have in our hands, in substantial integrity, the veritable Word of God.

—Sir Frederic Kenyon

Contents

Illustrations

Preface to the Third Edition

his study seeks to be a factual and honest account of how the Bible has been preserved and handed down to our generation. The subject is vast and at times complex. It has been my constant aim, therefore, to simplify the material and to state it, so far as possible, in a nontechnical manner. On the other hand, I have tried to get down to the heart of the question, for too many studies of this kind have been content with the mere citing of superficial facts about the Bible. These facts are important and interesting, of course, but they do not tell us *how* we got the Bible.

The third edition of this book now appears, more than fifteen years after the second edition. Much has happened since that time. In order to bring matters up to date and include other related information, I have completely rewritten almost everything in the book. Additions and changes have been made in every chapter, and five chapters of new material have been added. Readers of this edition will find new material especially on the Greek manuscripts, the Greek papyri, the Septuagint, the Latin Vulgate, the Latin manuscripts, the Hebrew manuscripts, the Dead Sea Scrolls, recent translations of the Bible, and more. Yet, with all these changes, I have tried to keep the book very much as it was from the first.

This third edition, as were its predecessors, is designed for the average reader. But the intention of the book all along has been that it be used for Bible classes, and thus the questions for discussion are an important part of this study. The teacher who leads in the study may find his or her task difficult. It will indeed be difficult unless due care and thought are given to each point. The teacher perhaps will wish to supplement the material by additional readings of selected books and articles in Bible dictionaries and encyclopedias. Both teacher and student should pay attention to the various articles and books referred to in the notes. Most of these are very readable and offer in effect a list of recommended readings.

Although this edition has been expanded to eighteen chapters, several of these may be studied together. If desirable, chapters 3 and 4 can be combined; other possible combinations include chapters 6 and 7, 8 and 9, 10 and 11, and 12 and 13. Nevertheless, each chapter stands on its own and covers significant information. Hopefully, each chapter will prove to be an interesting study in and of itself.

I add that the subject matter of this book, after many years, continues to fascinate me. As a young person, my own questions about the Bible prompted me to begin my own study. This quest was furthered by courses at Duke University under Dr. William H. Brownlee on the Dead Sea Scrolls and under Dr. Kenneth W. Clark on the textual criticism of the New Testament. Since then, study through the years has not only enhanced my interest but has resulted in building my own faith. I am grateful to God for the privilege of studying and teaching his Word.

My special thanks go to Mr. Don Stephenson and Baker Book House for inviting me to do this third edition as a fortieth-anniversary edition. My thanks also are due to Mr. Chad Allen of Baker Books for his editorial assistance and for his arranging the use of some of the photos at a time when I was unable to pursue it. And my thanks especially extend to the readers who have favorably received this book—though I am aware of its many shortcomings.

My hope is that this new edition may spark again studies of *How We Got the Bible*. May the Father in heaven enrich our understanding and appreciation of the Sacred Word that is able to instruct us for salvation.

Neil R. Lightfoot
Abilene Christian University
January 25, 2003

1

The Making of Ancient Books

ow the Bible has come down to us is a story of adventure and devotion. It is a story of toil and faith by those who, sometimes at great cost, passed down from generation to generation the message of salvation. The Bible did not just happen nor has it been preserved through the years by mere chance. Living in a day when books are written and printed by the thousands, we are apt to overlook the fascinating drama that lies behind our Bible.

How and when did the books of the Bible have their origin? In what sense are these books different from other books? How have these books been preserved and transmitted to us? These are some of the questions that arise in the mind of every thoughtful student of the Bible. The answers to these questions tell a story which spans thousands of years and takes us to various regions of the world and into the hearts of countless unnamed people whose first love was the Word of God.

The starting point of our Bible is preceded and determined by another story—the history of ancient books and writing. It is necessary to know this story because the Bible is composed of documents which were not only written long ago but have been transmitted and preserved through the years by means of writing. Knowing something of the early history of writing and the origin of ancient books will provide an interesting background for the history of the Bible and at the same time contribute immeasurably to an understanding of the life situations in which the Word of God had its birth.

Early Writing

Our Bible is a very old book, but it is by no means the oldest book in the world. Discoveries made in recent times show that writing was a well-established art in many countries long before the beginnings of the Hebrew nation in the land of Palestine. The earliest known examples of writing carry us into the ancient land of Egypt and Mesopotamia. We do not know exactly when or where writing began. Certainly no one sat down and said, "I am going to invent the art of writing." What we do know is that, as attested by an abundance of clay tablets, writing was widespread in Mesopotamia at least by 3000 B.C. We know also that Egyptian texts reach farther back and have survived in hieroglyphs on monuments, temples, and tombs.

Hieroglyphs are a form of picture writing based on a complicated system of consonants. The next logical step would have been an alphabetic script, but the Egyptians never took this step. As best as we can now surmise, somewhere between Egypt and Mesopotamia in the area of Syria-Palestine, some Semitic person(s) developed the alphabet. The time was perhaps about 1750 B.C., and from this first alphabet all other alphabets are derived.

The best example of an early alphabetic script are the so-called Proto-Sinaitic Inscriptions. Consisting of a small group of rock-carved graffiti and dating back to about 1500 B.C., these inscriptions are located only about fifty miles from the traditional site of Mount Sinai.

Such information as this has important implications for the origin of our Bible, for skeptical Bible critics formerly held that writing was unknown in the days of Moses and therefore that Moses could not have been the author of the first five books of the Bible. We now know that writing was practiced many centuries before Moses and that an alphabetic script was in use in the vicinity of Sinai. Indeed, at least five different systems of writing are known to have existed in the general area of Syria-Palestine when Moses lived.[1] All of this means it can no longer be assumed that it was impossible for Moses to have written the books ascribed to him.

Writing Materials

Ancient peoples of Palestine and adjoining countries adopted many kinds of materials for writing purposes. The Bible itself makes reference to a number of these.

1. Stone. In almost every region the earliest material on which writing has been found is stone. In Egypt and Mesopotamia the earliest inscriptions are on stone. In Babylonia and elsewhere, legal and religious laws were inscribed and erected for public display. Hammurabi (c. 1750 B.C.), one of the well-known Babylonian kings, set up his stele (an upright stone monument) in order that any oppressed person might read his 250 laws and be granted justice.

The oldest substantial portions of Hebrew writing found in Palestine are also on stone. The best examples of these are the Gezer Calendar and the Siloam Inscription. The Gezer Calendar is a kind of poem having to do with various agricultural activities during the months of the year. Scratched on a small piece of white limestone are twenty words of an early Hebrew alphabetic script, dating from the time of Solomon (c. 925 B.C.). The Siloam Inscription goes back to about 700 B.C., when King Hezekiah had a tunnel constructed to convey water into Jerusalem (2 Kings 20:20; 2 Chron. 32:30). The inscription tells of the successful completion of the S-shaped tunnel dug from opposite ends.[2]

Another well-known inscription which has survived is the Moabite Stone, found in the area east of the Dead Sea. Containing thirty-four lines of "Canaanite" script, written in the ninth century B.C., it was erected by King Mesha of Moab to commemorate his revolt against Israel (2 Kings 3:4–27). It is the only inscription outside of Palestine proper that mentions the Divine Name (YHWH) of Israel's God.[3]

That these early specimens of writing exist on stone is in remarkable agreement with the Bible account, for the earliest writing material mentioned in the Old Testament is stone. The Ten Commandments, as almost everyone knows, were first written on stone. The Book of Exodus reads, "And he gave to Moses, when he had made an end of speaking with him upon Mount Sinai, the two tables of the testimony, tables of stone written with the finger of God" (Exod. 31:18; cf. Exod. 34:1, 28; Deut. 10:1–5).

Connected with stone are texts that were written with ink on plaster. Moses had said to the Israelites, "On the day you cross over the Jordan into the land that the Lord your God is giving you, you shall set up large stones and cover them with plaster. You shall write on them all the words of this law. . . ." (Deut. 27:2–3). And Joshua had done this (Josh. 8:22).

Two inscriptions of this kind, ink on plaster, have been discovered rather recently. One of these is of particular interest. It is an Aramaic text from the plaster of a temple wall in the Jordan valley. The first line of the text reads, "This is the record of Balaam, son of Beor. . . ." Although this clearly is a reference to the Biblical Balaam (Numbers 22–24), the inscription is noteworthy for another reason. Consisting of a number of straight lines, its appearance is like a column of a scroll. Its upper and left margins are ruled and its headings are in red ink. Dated about 700 B.C., this is something of what a book looked like in the time of the prophet Isaiah.[4]

2. Clay. The most common writing material in Mesopotamia was clay. The moist clay was made into tablets, then written upon and baked in an oven or allowed to dry in the sun. This is the kind of material referred to in Ezekiel 4:1 when the prophet is commanded to sketch a plan of Jerusalem on a brick. Clay tablets were so durable that a half million or more of them have survived to modern times.

Clay tablets were written upon in cuneiform (wedge-shaped) letters. Tablets were made in all shapes and sizes and were used for all types of literary purposes. Historical texts, often in the shape of a barrel, were placed in the cornerstones of buildings, and clay nails were stuck in the walls, inscribed in the king's name in whose time the building was erected. Long literary texts were continued from tablet to tablet, sometimes requiring numerous tablets to make one "book." The tablets were kept in special archive rooms, stored on shelves or in baskets or boxes or clay jars (cf. Jer. 32:14).[5]

The use of clay tablets spread to other parts of the world. Recently, Ebla in Syria has drawn much attention. In Ebla a whole library of some 16,000 tablets has been unearthed—royal edicts and letters, treatises, hymns to gods, and so forth. The tablets, which may date as far back as 2400 B.C., are written in cuneiform in the "Eblaite" language.[6]

Previous discoveries of large numbers of tablets have proved to be of great importance. At Tell-el-Amarna, in central Egypt, a native woman found several hundred tablets inscribed in cuneiform. From about 1350 B.C., the tablets turned out to be the official correspondence between the pharaohs of Egypt and rulers in Palestine, Syria, Mesopotamia, and other places. At Ras Shamra (ancient Ugarit) in Syria, hundreds of cuneiform tablets were found, dating from about the same time.

The chronicles of a number of kings mentioned in the Old Testament have been preserved on clay tablets. Sargon II claims the capture of Samaria (721 B.C.), while a little later (701 B.C.) Sennacherib details the siege of Hezekiah in Jerusalem. Ashurbanipal, known as Osnapper in the Old Testament (Ezra 4:10), boasts that he had learned "the entire art of writing on clay tablets."[7] It was he who sent out his scribes to copy and translate into Assyrian all the books they could find, thousands of which have survived and are now housed in the British Museum in London. Nebuchadrezzar II, usually known as Nebuchadnezzar, relates how he rebuilt the city of Babylon. Of his writings that remain, most of them relate to his extensive building accomplishments (cf. Dan. 4:28–30). Belshazzar, mentioned in the Book of Daniel, left clay cylinders of prayers and tablets on various subjects.

3. Wood and wax. The Old Testament makes specific reference to writing on wooden rods and sticks (Num. 17:2–3; Ezek. 37:16–17). In Greek and Roman times a whitened board was used for public notices, and this was called an "album." At the

death of Jesus, the inscription on the cross was probably written on a whitewashed board.

Wooden tablets often had an inlay of wax, which could be written upon or erased as occasion demanded. The Assyrians used such tablets, and they were especially popular with the Romans. These were their "notebooks." They could be used singly or fastened together and turned like pages of a book. The Romans called a tablet bound together a "codex" (plural "codices"), the term that was later employed for a book with many sheets. Isaiah 30:8 and Habakkuk 2:2 may well refer to these wooden writing boards.

4. Metal. Gold as a writing surface is referred to in Exodus 28: 36. Cuneiform writings were made on gold, silver, copper, and bronze, on plaques or tablets of these metals. In Greece and Rome government records of treaties and decrees were frequently inscribed on bronze tablets. Roman soldiers, at the time of their discharge, were presented with small bronze tablets called "diplomas," granting them special privileges and citizenship.

Of special interest are two small silver scrolls worn as amulets around the neck. One contains the priestly blessing that reads, "May the Lord bless and keep you. May the Lord cause his face to shine upon you and give you peace" (Num. 6:24–26). The inscription in old Hebrew letters is from the sixth century B.C. and is the earliest known that contains words of Scripture.[8]

5. Ostraca. In contrast to expensive metals was the widespread use of ostraca or potsherds as a writing material. Broken pottery was readily available and was used in antiquity very much as we use scrap paper. Large numbers of ostraca have come from Egypt, representing many stages of its history. Two sherds have been found with the name of Narmer, the first Pharaoh of Egypt (c. 3100 B.C.), on them.

In Palestine, one sherd has been discovered with the name of Pekah, king of Israel about 735 B.C., on it. Another sherd has been found and dates back to about 1100 B.C. It contains, with minor differences, the Hebrew alphabet of twenty-two letters.[9] Likewise, the Samaria ostraca and Lachish letters are of special importance. The Samaria ostraca are notations of goods received at the royal palace, probably from the time of

Jeroboam II (c. 750 B.C.). The Lachish letters are part of the correspondence of an officer at Lachish and a subordinate elsewhere, when the little kingdom of Judah was under attack by Nebuchadnezzar of Babylon. The letters frequently employ the Divine Name. One letter begins, "May YHWH cause my lord to hear tidings of peace."[10]

Ostraca as writing surfaces have proved to be practically indestructible. Twenty-five or more ostraca have been found with short passages of the New Testament inscribed on them. Earlier, in the fifth century B.C., the people of Athens "ostracized" their unpopular fellow citizens by writing the names of those to be banished on ostraca.

6. Papyrus. A long list of other writing materials used by the ancients could be drawn up, but all of these materials, including those discussed thus far, have distinct disadvantages. Some could bear only a few words, others were bulky and heavy. In the case of clay, for instance, a lengthy text would require a wheelbarrow of tablets. It is no wonder, then, that the ancient world came to rely more and more on a light, flexible writing material known as papyrus.

The Book of Job asks, "Can papyrus grow where there is no marsh?" (8:11). In Egypt, along the Nile River, where marshes and swamps remained after the river's annual flood, this was the ideal place for papyrus to grow and flourish. For long centuries the papyrus plant was the symbol of Lower (Northern) Egypt. Its eminent position is represented today in tomb paintings and by temple columns beautifully shaped like flowering papyrus stalks.

The Egyptians used papyrus as a writing material from about 3000 B.C. They used it for many other purposes as well, for fuel, food, boats, ropes, baskets, sandals, clothing, and even for tables and chairs.[11] The Bible speaks of "vessels of papyrus" (Isa. 18:2); "skiffs of reed" (Job 9:26); and, in reference to the infant Moses, "a basket of bulrushes," which probably refers to papyrus. "Civilization," Pliny said, "depends on the use of papyrus."

Pliny lived in the first century A.D. and has left an important account of how strips of papyrus were transformed into "paper." "Paper is made from the papyrus plant by separating it with a needle point into very thin strips as broad as possible. The choice quality comes from the center, and thence in the order of slicing."[12] Pliny goes on to relate how strips of papyrus were laid crosswise, trimmed and pressed together, and then dried in the sun. When rough spots were smoothed out, the result was a polished paper of different qualities.

The popularity of papyrus spread from Egypt to surrounding countries, and its use was so general that it became the universal medium for the making of books in Greece and Rome. We are quite sure the letters and books of the New Testament were written at first on papyrus. This is clearly the case in 2 John 12 where "paper" (Greek, *chartes*) refers to papyrus.

From the world of the once flourishing papyrus has descended to modern times a vocabulary of terms that remains. Papyrus, of course, is the origin of our word "paper." "Papyrology" is the science that deals especially with writings on papyrus. The Greek word *chartes* denotes a sheet or roll of papyrus, with the term appearing in Latin as *charta*, and in English as "chart," "charter," and "card." The word *biblos* was a Greek term for papyrus. *Biblion,* the related word, was the ordinary word for "papyrus roll"; *biblia,* the plural for "papyrus rolls," meant simply "the books." It was but another step to refer to "the books" as "the Books" and then to "the Book" of Sacred Scripture. Thus the word "Bible" itself goes back to the papyrus plant.

7. Leather and parchment. It used to be common to credit Eumenes II, king of Pergamum shortly after 200 B.C., with the invention of parchment. Eumenes was building up his library to rival the great library of King Ptolemy in Alexandria. The king of Egypt moved to cut off the supply of papyrus to Pergamum, and in response Eumenes was forced to develop "parchment." This story is untrue if taken in the sense that Eumenes was the first to make use of parchment or leather; for long before the second century, animal skins for writing were unquestionably in use. In Egypt, for example, mention is made of leather documents as far back as 2500 B.C. Many leather rolls have been found in Egypt and in other countries as well. So Eumenes was by no means the first to use animal skins for writing, although he may have developed and perfected a better

process for treating the skins. Whatever the case, Pergamum and parchment are indisputably connected, the word "parchment" being derived from the Greek term *pergamene*.

There is a difference, however, between leather and parchment, depending on how the animal skins are treated. Both leather and parchment are dehaired and soaked in lime water, but leather is tanned by the application of chemical reagents, while parchment is stretched and dried on a frame. The skins are mainly from small animals such as sheep, goats, and calves. Strictly speaking, "vellum" (related to the English word *veal*) refers to calfskin, but the term is also applied to other fine skins. Generally, however, "vellum" and "parchment" are used interchangeably to describe a smooth, thin writing surface of any skin.

The Old Testament makes no direct reference to writing on leather. In recent times numerous manuscripts from the Dead Sea area came to light, and most of them were written on leather.[13] The Jewish Talmud, a code of traditional laws, required explicitly that the Torah (Law) be copied on animal skins, a regulation that undoubtedly embodies an ancient tradition. It is safe to conclude, therefore, that the Old Testament writings were regularly copied on prepared skins. When in New Testament times the Apostle Paul requests that "the parchments" be sent to him (2 Tim. 4:13), perhaps he is speaking of portions of the Old Testament.

Parchment as a writing surface gained ground slowly, yet its final triumph over papyrus was inevitable. Papyrus is not as durable as parchment and in time became less and less available. So from the fourth century through the Middle Ages the principal receptacle for the written Word of God was parchment.

Summary

The history of writing leads back to the remote past. Writing was being practiced widely hundreds of years before the time of Moses. It is not a foregone conclusion that Moses could not have written some parts of our Bible. As in our day, people wrote long ago on almost all kinds of materials, depending on their locale and situation in history. For the Old Testament the most important writing material was leather. At the time when the New Testament was penned, papyrus was in general use. In about the fourth century, parchment displaced papyrus, and so the vast majority of ancient New Testament manuscripts that survive today are written on the handsome and durable material of vellum or parchment.

For Discussion

1. What information is available to show that writing was generally practiced before the time of Moses? Of what significance is this information on the authorship of the first five books of the Bible?
2. What were some of the main materials used in ancient times for writing? Which of these materials was the most important for the Old Testament?
3. The Bible makes reference to a number of writing materials. Check back over these references. What discoveries mentioned in this chapter shed light on what we know about the Bible?
4. Illustrate the importance of papyrus for the ancient world. What is its significance for the early history of the New Testament?
5. What is parchment? What is the story behind its development? What is vellum? Is it to be distinguished from parchment?

2

The Birth of the Bible

t is impossible to say how or when and under what circumstances the Bible had its origin. As through hundreds of years ancient literary works took shape in many forms, so also from century to century the many books of the Bible were coming into being separately and under varying conditions. The Bible is a collection of books, which is indicated whenever we use the term *Bible*. The term, as we have seen, is derived from *biblia*, literally "the books." But the Bible is more than an ordinary collection: it is a treasure-house of sacred books which has grown through the centuries until it has attained its present stature. And it is the firm belief of the Christian that the Bible is honored today because in the past it grew under the favorable and directing influence of Him who is the Author of all things.

The Codex

Before going further, however, something more needs to be said about the form of ancient books. Wherever the use of papyrus and leather prevailed, for many centuries the form of the book was the roll or scroll. In the case of papyrus, the roll was made by gluing the sheets end to end. Usually all the writing was done on one side, although at times a scribe might make use of both sides of the roll (cf. Rev. 5:1). The writing was arranged in columns, each about three or four inches wide. The rolls varied in size, ordinarily no longer than thirty-five feet and about nine to ten inches high.

The length of a roll has some importance for the New Testament. A roll of thirty-two to thirty-five feet would be needed for a more lengthy book such as Matthew or Luke or Acts. (That rolls rarely exceeded this length might account for Luke and Acts being written as separate volumes.) It follows, then, that so long as the roll remained in use, each of the Gospels and Acts, and perhaps some of the longer letters, would have to circulate individually.

But just as the use of papyrus gave way to parchment, the roll form of book gave way to the codex. "Codex," as we have seen, was the term for the Roman writing tablet, and it is also the term that came to be used for a book with leaves—a "book" in the modern sense of the term.

It has been said that the inventor of the codex belongs with other nameless benefactors of mankind such as the inventor of the wheel and the deviser of the alphabet.[1] The reader of a roll held the roll horizontally, unrolling it with one hand and rolling it up with the other. In the best hands the procedure was somewhat awkward. The codex was much more convenient to use. In the making of a codex, the sheets were placed together, folded in the middle and stitched, then opened in separate pages. The result was a book that could be easily read, easily referred to, and easily carried about. It could be written on both sides of the pages and could even be bound to include several books in one. For these reasons, Christians especially found the codex advantageous, for it allowed them, say, to make one book for the Four Gospels, another for Paul's letters, and later one book for the entire Bible.

At first the codex was of papyrus, then subsequently of parchment. The early codex was quite simple in form, all the sheets being folded clumsily together. Later, four sheets were put together to make a "quire," a term that now stands for any number of sheets gathered together. Parchment sheets were arranged for a desired visual effect, with the coarser "hair side" facing another hair side and the smoother "flesh side" facing another flesh side.

When did the codex displace the roll? And who was responsible for it? The whole subject has been thoroughly explored in recent years.[2] More and more it seems that the codex may very well be a Christian innovation. If not, we know at least that Christians were the first to make extensive use of the codex.[3] Our earliest extant texts of the New Testament characteristically are written in a codex. By the time of the second century, the use of the codex among Christians was so universal that its introduction must have taken place by or before A.D. 90.

The Early Form of the Bible

The Bible has reached its present stature through gradual and almost imperceptible stages of growth. According to the Bible, at first God's communication with humankind was oral; God spoke directly to such men as Adam and Noah and Abraham. But the time came when it was necessary for the divine will to be put into more permanent form and that a record of God's revelations be made for succeeding generations. In other words, it was God's purpose that by means of a *written record* he would be revealed to all ages and tongues as Creator and Redeemer.

The first person mentioned in the Bible as writing anything is Moses, who lived perhaps as early as 1500 B.C.[4] In the early books of the Bible six distinct writings are attributed to his hand: (1) the memorial concerning Amalek (Exod. 17:14); (2) the words of the covenant made at Sinai (Exod. 24:4); (3) the Ten Commandments (Exod. 34:27–28); (4) the journeys of the children of Israel in the wilderness (Num. 33:2); (5) the Book of the Law, which was to be kept with the Ark of the Covenant (Deut. 31:9, 24); and (6) the Song found in Deuteronomy 32: 1–43 (Deut. 31:22). In addition, Moses is held by strict Jewish tradition as being the author of the first five books of the Bible known as the Pentateuch. Other writers of the Bible, and the

Lord himself, give unvarying support to this view (cf. Josh. 8:31; 2 Kings 14:6; Ezra 6:18; Mark 12:26; Luke 2:22; John 7:19).

When divine revelation was put in writing, it was natural for other revelations and events to be recorded. So the successor of Moses, Joshua, also wrote words "in the book of the law of God" (Josh. 24:26). This in turn became the practice of other men of God who wrote both history and prophecy (cf. 1 Sam. 10:25; Jer. 36:2), with the result that later generations are found consulting the writings of their esteemed predecessors (cf. Dan. 9:2; Neh. 8:1). In this way the Old Testament Scriptures grew gradually and came to be assembled into an accepted collection about the time of Ezra (c. 400 B.C.). The Jewish authority, Josephus, said that no book was added to the Hebrew Scriptures after the time of Malachi.[5]

The New Testament came into being gradually also, although the books themselves were written in a comparatively short period of time (A.D. 50–100). The books were mostly letters penned by inspired men and addressed to different churches and individuals. From the first, however, they were looked upon as distinctively authoritative writings; thus they were received with respect and read in the public assemblies (1 Thess. 5:27). Soon afterward came the interchange of extant letters among the churches (cf. Col. 4:16), the individual churches in this way profiting from an exchange of apostolic instructions.

The next step was the embodiment in writing of the central events of the life of Jesus. At first oral accounts of his work by eyewitnesses filled the needs of the infant church, but as years passed eyewitness accounts became few and insufficient. Now the demand was for authoritative written narratives, and in fulfillment of this demand Matthew, Mark, Luke, and John sent out their witness to Jesus (cf. Luke 1:1–4; John 20:30–31). The logical outgrowth of the Four Gospels was the Book of Acts, which told the story of the primitive church. As a kind of climax to the whole came Revelation with its prospect of a triumphant Christ. The result of it all was that a new community of people, just like the people of the Old Covenant, had as a cherished treasure their own writings as "Scripture."

The Form of Our Bible Today

Our Bible today is divided into two major sections known as the Old and New Testaments. The term "testament" is an unfortunate translation (Greek, *diatheke*) and would be better rendered as "covenant." Thus the basic structure of the Bible hinges on the idea that God has made two significant covenants with his people and that the New Covenant has displaced the Old.

The Old Covenant appears in our English Bibles in the following arrangement: (1) five books of Law or the Pentateuch (Genesis to Deuteronomy); (2) twelve books of History (Joshua to Esther); (3) five books of Poetry (Job to Song of Solomon); and (4) seventeen books of Prophets (Isaiah to Malachi), sometimes subdivided into five books of Major Prophets and twelve books of Minor Prophets. This arrangement of Old Testament books found in English Bibles is derived from the Latin Vulgate translation, which in turn is derived from the Septuagint or Greek version.

The books of the Hebrew Bible, however, are grouped differently, as follows:

1. Law: Genesis, Exodus, Leviticus, Numbers, Deuteronomy
2. Prophets:
   a. Former Prophets: Joshua, Judges, 1 and 2 Samuel, 1 and 2 Kings
   b. Latter Prophets: Isaiah, Jeremiah, Ezekiel, and the Book of the Twelve
3. Writings: Psalms, Proverbs, Job, Song of Solomon, Ruth, Lamentations, Ecclesiastes, Esther, Daniel, Ezra, Nehemiah, and 1 and 2 Chronicles

If we compare this arrangement with our English Bible, we see that the Hebrew Bible has but three major divisions: the Law, the Prophets, and the Writings (cf. Luke 24:44). There are other differences as well. The twelve Minor Prophets are taken together as one book and are known as the Twelve. Another difference appears by terming Joshua, Judges, and the Books of Samuel and Kings as Former Prophets. These books, which we regard as historical, are known as prophetic because they were written with a prophetic outlook by men who most likely were prophets. However different the arrangement, it is important to remember that the books included in Protestant English Bibles are precisely the same as found in the Hebrew Bible.

The books of the New Covenant are grouped together in three parts: (1) five books of History (Matthew to Acts), (2) twenty-one books of Doctrine (Romans to Jude), and (3) one book of Prophecy (Revelation).

1. The five books of History may be further divided into the Four Gospels and Acts of the Apostles. The Gospels are so called because they present the message of God's news revealed in Jesus Christ. In a larger sense they may be referred to as lives of Jesus, but in the strict sense they are not biographies but mere sketches of some of the great teachings and achievements of that unique Life. The first three Gospels are known as the Synoptic Gospels because of their similar contents. The Gospel of John was probably written at a later date and seems to presuppose a knowledge of many events in Jesus' life. The Acts of the Apostles is a kind of continuation of the Gospel of Luke, and because of their interconnection, they are sometimes referred to as Luke-Acts.

2. The twenty-one books of Doctrine are letters written by various inspired men. The first thirteen in this group bear the name of Paul. The Pauline letters are of two groups: those written before his two years' imprisonment in Rome (cf. Acts 28:30) and those written later (1 and 2 Timothy and Titus), which are sometimes called the Pastoral Epistles. The Book of Hebrews is sometimes numbered in the Pauline group, although its authorship remains a question mark.

3. The one book of Prophecy, the Book of Revelation or Apocalypse, suitably appears at the end of the Bible since it summarizes in symbolic language the principles revealed in preceding books and at the same time gives a prophetic foretaste of things to come.

The Languages of the Bible

We turn next to the languages in which the various books of the Bible were originally composed. Our English translations are beautiful literary works in themselves, but it will aid the Bible student immeasurably to know something of the Bible languages. A knowledge of these languages will also provide another link in the history of the Bible.

The Bible was written originally in three languages: (1) Hebrew, (2) Aramaic, and (3) Greek. These languages are by no means dead languages. Hebrew is the spoken language of the state of Israel; Aramaic is spoken in Syria and a few other areas; and Greek, of course, is spoken by millions of people today, although modern Greek is quite different from the Greek of the New Testament.

1. Hebrew. Almost all the books of the Old Testament are written in Hebrew. Hebrew comes from a large family of languages called "Semitic" and is akin to such languages as Aramaic, Syriac, Akkadian (Assyrian-Babylonian), and Arabic. To people of the Western hemisphere, Hebrew is a "strange" language. It is written "backwards" (from right to left), has many sounds that are foreign to ears accustomed to English forms, and possesses a vocabulary that is unrelated to English words. (The King James and American Standard reader can turn to Psalm 119, the sections of which are numbered according to Hebrew letters, and get a sample of the Hebrew alphabet.) In addition, the Hebrew alphabet is without vowels. It is true that a system of vowel-points has been added which gives untold aid in the study of the language, but to a person thoroughly trained in the language this vowel system often proves a hindrance as much as a help. Modern Hebrew books and magazines are normally printed without vowels, and this is precisely the way the Old Testament text originally appeared.

2. Aramaic. Aramaic is a kindred language to Hebrew and after the time of the exile (c. 500 B.C.) became the common tongue in Palestine. (Nehemiah 8:8 is usually read with the assumption that the people did not know pure Hebrew and therefore needed a translation into the familiar Aramaic.)

Because Aramaic was spoken by the Jews several centuries before Christ, it is not surprising to find some portions of the Old Testament in Aramaic instead of Hebrew. Aramaic sections of the Old Testament include two words as a place name in Genesis 31:47; one verse in Jeremiah 10:11; about six chapters in the Book of Daniel (2:4b–7:28); and several chapters in Ezra (4:8–6:18; 7:12–26). If someone looks at a copy of the Hebrew Bible, these sections in Aramaic will appear no different from other parts of the Old Testament. This is true because the Aramaic characters are like those of the Hebrew, or, to be more exact, the square-shaped Hebrew letters are actually borrowed from the Aramaic. So there is no difference in appearance between Hebrew and Aramaic, but the two are distinct languages.

The longest Old Testament section in Aramaic begins in Daniel 2:4. The first part of this verse is in Hebrew, and the Aramaic portion starts with the response of the Chaldeans, "O king, live forever!" An interesting confirmation of this linguistic change within the verse has come to light in recent years. The amazing Dead Sea Scrolls have produced a little fragment of this section of Daniel, and in the middle of Daniel 2:4 the Hebrew stops and the Aramaic begins exactly as our text reads two thousand years later. The Hebrew portion of Daniel resumes at the end of chapter 7. This transition of Aramaic to Hebrew is also confirmed by the Dead Sea Scrolls, for of the two manuscripts that have this section, both have the change from Aramaic to Hebrew precisely where our modern text has it!

Aramaic continued for centuries as the vernacular of Palestine. The New Testament preserves for us Aramaic expressions of Jesus, such as *talitha cumi* ("Little girl, get up.") in Mark 5:41; *ephphatha* ("Be opened.") in Mark 7:34; and *Eloi, Eloi, lama sabachthani* ("My God, my God, why has thou forsaken me?") in Mark 15:34 (cf. Matt. 27:46). Jesus habitually addressed God as Abba (Aramaic for "Father"), which did not fail to leave its mark on the vocabulary of the early church (cf. Rom. 8:15; Gal. 6:4). Another common phrase of early Christians was *Maran atha*, which means "Our Lord, come!" (1 Cor. 16:22). These expressions clearly show that the language normally spoken by our Lord and his Jewish followers was Aramaic.

3. Greek. Although the spoken language of Jesus was Aramaic, the books that comprise our New Testament were written in Greek. There is little question today on this point, although a few scholars have maintained that some portions of the New Testament were issued at first in Aramaic. It was in the providence of God, since the gospel was to be proclaimed to every creature, that the New Testament writers made use of a language that was known throughout the Mediterranean world. Greek in the first century, as English is today, was the "universal" language.

The Greek of the New Testament exhibits certain linguistic peculiarities. For a long time it was affirmed that these peculiarities could be explained on no other basis than the supposition of a "Holy Ghost Greek." Recent discoveries and research have wholly overthrown this supposition, and now the language of the New Testament is more correctly termed "Hellenistic" or *"Koine"* (common) Greek. We have been brought to this unmistakable conclusion largely because of discoveries among the ancient Greek papyri. Their impact on the New Testament text and its vocabulary will be considered later.

These papyri were written by ordinary people in colloquial Greek. This Greek of the marketplace appears in the New Testament, but by and large its language is more literary than spoken Greek. In addition, the Greek New Testament has ingrained in it a peculiar Jewish or Semitic element. Most of its authors were Jews, who often thought and wrote in Semitic idiom. This is noticeable even to the English reader in such expressions as "truly *[amen]* I say to you," "it came to pass," "behold," "and . . . and,"—expressions that are characteristically Semitic. In addition, the New Testament authors give a distinctive "Christian" flavor to ordinary Greek words. Such words are numerous, including "love," "grace," "peace," "faith," "humility," "life," "gospel," "salvation," "justification," "apostle," "church," and so forth. The Greek of the New Testament possesses features all its own.[6]

"In Praise of Ancient Scribes"

The remaining portion of this chapter will take a brief look at ancient scribes. If we can learn more about them, surely this will help us appreciate what they have handed down to us.

It is scarcely possible to overstate the importance of early scribes. In Mesopotamia and in Egypt, the trained scribe was highly prized. In Palestine, professional scribes were responsible for writing and copying most Hebrew documents.

The Romans, as the Greeks before them, gave their energies to producing and selling books. Numbers of scribes worked simultaneously and copied their works by dictation. Publishers advertised "best-sellers" and pushed circulation of their books throughout the Empire. All of this testifies to an enormous amount of scribal activity in the ancient world.

The earliest copies of Christian writings were probably made for the local church by some member of the congregation. As the number of Christians grew, it was necessary to have more and more copies for new converts and for translations into other languages.

If it were possible to be at a scribe's side or look over his shoulder, what would we see? To begin with, the scribe would not be sitting in a chair at a table or desk. If he was taking brief notes, he might be standing. If he was copying a manuscript, he probably would be sitting on a bench or stool, perhaps with something under his feet to raise his legs, with the codex laid across his knees.[7]

The scribe's pen was a reed, sharpened and slit to form a nib. His ink was a carbon ink, black in color, made from soot mixed with water and gum. Later, a metallic ink of various colors was used. His other equipment included a stylus and a ruler for the making of lines on his parchment; a sponge for the making of erasures and wiping off his pen; a penknife to sharpen the pen; and a piece of pumice to smooth his pen or his writing surface.

Texts on papyrus and parchment were written in one or more columns, depending on the size of the codex. Before beginning to write, the scribe would draw lines on his sheet, serving to mark off the required margins and to guide his pen as he wrote. These colorless lines, made by dragging a stylus over the parchment, were hardly noticeable to the reader of the finished manuscript.

The Romans, as we have seen, met the urgent demand for books by employing scribes who copied by dictation. This practice was continued by many Christian scribes. In making multiple copies, scribes wrote in a writing room or "scriptorium," listening to the reader as he read aloud from his text. When this practice began we do not know. But we do know that in the third century Origen had a scriptorium in Caesarea and that he was furnished with a team of stenographers who copied by dictation. Origen's scholarship gave impetus to the great Christian library at Caesarea in the next century. Undoubtedly, similar libraries existed in the main centers of Biblical research.[8]

During the Middle Ages, scribes, working in the scriptoria of monasteries, were the book producers of all sorts of literary works. By transcribing ancient texts, the scribes kept aglow the lamp of knowledge and especially contributed to the preservation of texts of Scripture.

Scribes sometimes wrote notes in their margins or at the end of their manuscripts, telling us something about their work. An end note, or colophon, might include the scribe's name, and occasionally the place and date he finished the manuscript. Some notes attest to the great labor involved. One scribe tells of completing his manuscript "with great sweat and toil." Others just exclaim: "The end of the book—thanks be to God!"[9]

Alan R. Millard, a specialist in Semitic languages, has written an excellent article entitled "In Praise of Ancient Scribes."[10] The purpose of his article is to show with what care ancient scribes did their work. Such scribes, he reminds us, deserve our praise.

Summary

Our Bible is a collection of extraordinary books written over a period of fourteen or fifteen hundred years. The Bible gradually grew until its completion near the close of the first century A.D. As a collection of books, the Bible has been arranged in various ways through the years. The order of books in our English Old Testament basically goes back to the Greek version, which was widely used in the early church. Our New Testament writings are arranged according to a logical pattern, although different orders can be found among various manuscripts. The languages of the Bible are three in number: Hebrew, Aramaic, and Greek. Some of the Old Testament was written in Aramaic, but Hebrew was the predominant language. By the time of the first century, Greek had become a worldwide language, which accounts for the New Testament being written in Greek. But we would not have a Bible at all without the amazing work of the scribes.

For Discussion

1. What is a codex? How does it compare with a book in roll form? When and by whom was the codex introduced? Can we be certain of this?
2. Who is mentioned in the Bible as being the first author of anything? What evidence is available to show that he is the author of the Pentateuch?
3. At about what time were the books of the New Testament written? How does this compare to the interval of time during which the Old Testament books originated?
4. Describe the arrangement of Old Testament books in the English Bible. How does this compare to the Hebrew arrangement? Are the books the same in each?
5. What are the three main divisions of the New Testament? Which writer is responsible for the largest group of New Testament books?
6. Name the three original languages in which the Bible was written. In what language was the New Testament written? What was the language normally spoken by Jesus? How do we know this?
7. Why were scribes so important in (1) the ancient world and (2) the Middle Ages? What do you remember about how they did their work?

3

Manuscripts of the New Testament

e have seen that the New Testament books made their appearance in the latter half of the first century. These books were undoubtedly written on papyrus sheets which, with constant use, might not last as long as a decade. So not long after the New Testament was written, the original autographs perished. Yet God's Word was not hopelessly lost. The various New Testament letters had been received with the authority of heaven behind them, which prompted early Christians to make many copies of these precious apostolic messages. These copies of the New Testament in Greek are known simply as "manuscripts." (The word "manuscript" denotes anything written by hand, but by general consent in connection with the Bible the term is restricted to the documents of the original tongues. Thus a New Testament manuscript is a *Greek* manuscript.)

Let us suppose that we have a New Testament manuscript before our eyes. The first thing to learn about it is its age. How old is it? Of course, the age of many manuscripts is easily attainable, for several hundred have dates on them that indicate the exact day and year they were copied. These dated manuscripts are of great assistance in determining the age of manuscripts without dates. How, then, are undated manuscripts dated? In seeking answers here, we must look carefully at the handwriting. Are the letters large or small? Are the words all written together or are they separated? How many columns are there to a page, and what is the appearance of the columns? Are there any marks of punctuation or divisions into paragraphs? What is the form of the letters? Are they plain and simple or elaborate and complex? These are some of the basic questions to ask when one examines a manuscript. A trained specialist will observe many other things and with technical knowledge and experience can come to a reliable determination of the date of almost any manuscript. There are exceptions, to be sure, and sometimes the most perplexing problems have to do with dating the later manuscripts.[1]

New Testament manuscripts are of two major types. The manuscripts of one group, the earliest and certainly the most important, are written in capital letters and are known as "uncials." The handwriting found in a larger group is smaller and more cursivelike in appearance; these manuscripts are known as "cursives" or "minuscules." (The word "minuscule" means "small" and refers to a handwritten book in small letters that often were written cursively.) The minuscules did not make their debut until the ninth century and thus are of less value.

The number of our New Testament manuscripts is vast, more than 5,300 in all. Not all of these, however, contain the complete text of the New Testament. In fact, only a few contain anything like what can be termed a complete New Testament. Yet the New Testament is without doubt the best-attested book from the ancient world. Most of the manuscripts do not contain the entire New Testament for the simple reason that a hand-produced copy of the whole was too bulky for practical use.

Our present manuscripts indicate that when making copies of the New Testament, early Christians produced manuscripts that fit more or less within one of four categories: (1) the Four Gospels, (2) Acts and the General Epistles, (3) the Pauline Epistles, and (4) the Book of Revelation. At first, however, the individual writings probably circulated separately, then were joined with others of like kind, and finally were combined into one of the four standard groups. Therefore, it is not surprising that most of our manuscripts today do not contain all of the New Testament books. Of the known 5,300 manuscripts, the vast majority are minuscules that date from the ninth to the sixteenth century, while those of uncial script number altogether about 650.

When the New Testament was first written, both uncial and cursive styles of handwriting were in use. The various letters of the New Testament were probably dictated (Rom. 16:22; 1 Peter 5:12; cf. Gal. 6:11), and this may mean that at first they were written cursively. Before long, however, they were copied as books with a book hand, that is, in uncial script. Uncial manuscripts are those in large letters without intervening spaces between the words and with scarcely any marks of punctuation. The way Paul's Epistle to the Romans appeared in uncial characters may be illustrated as follows:

PAULASERVANTOFJESUSCHRISTCALLEDTOBE
ANAPOSTLESETAPARTFORTHEGOSPELOFGODW
HICHHEPROMISEDBEFOREHANDTHROUGHHISP

We do not know how Paul's original dictated letter looked. Perhaps it looked something like the above, probably written more cursively and possibly with abbreviations for familiar words. Of course, Paul wrote in Greek instead of English. Notice also that in uncials an unfinished word was completed on the line below in order to keep the columns straight.

The uncial hand is represented in about 650 manuscripts. This number includes about 95 papyri and more than 270 lectionaries. Lectionaries are manuscripts especially designed for reading in public worship. The papyri, which mainly have come to light in the twentieth century, are of immense importance for the text of the New Testament. We will consider them in more detail later. Excluding the above numbers, this means that about 280 uncial manuscripts copied on parchment are extant, and these date from the third or fourth century to the tenth century. But the above figures are not precise, because some manuscripts that once were counted separately are now known to be parts of others.

The large number of New Testament manuscripts has necessitated a system by which they can be identified. The most commonly used system, especially for the better-known manuscripts, goes back to the eighteenth century and was originated by J. J. Wettstein. This system designates uncial manuscripts with capital letters and minuscule manuscripts with Arabic numerals. But there are serious drawbacks to this procedure, not the least of which is that now there are more known uncials than letters of the alphabet(s) (including the Latin, Greek, and Hebrew alphabets). In 1908 an updated system was introduced by C. R. Gregory, which designates all manuscripts with numbers and distinguishes uncials with an initial zero, as in 0220. But for our purposes the older system will suffice. The following descriptions of manuscripts will include the identifying letter or number.

The Important Uncials

By and large the most important copies of the Scriptures are the oldest. Here we are very fortunate indeed, for among the very valuable papyri are about fifty that date from the second to the fourth century. In addition, our oldest vellum manuscripts are complete or almost complete copies of the New Testament and have practically all of the Old Testament as well. These old copies are three in number and are known as the Vatican, the Sinaitic, and the Alexandrian Manuscripts. They date back to A.D. 300–450. Aged, worn, faded, and unattractive in many respects, these are the greatest documentary treasures in Christendom—the oldest Bibles in the world!

1. The Vatican Manuscript (B). This fourth-century manuscript is acknowledged widely as being the most important witness on the text of the New Testament. As its name implies, it is located in the Vatican Library in Rome. It has resided there at least since 1481, the date of a catalog in which it is listed. But the library was founded in 1448, and the manuscript may have been one of the original volumes of the collection.

Sir Frederic Kenyon has pointed out that, although there is no story to tell of the manuscript's discovery, an interesting story does exist concerning the efforts of many scholars to publish its contents. Not until the close of the last century did the exact contents of the manuscript become available. Kenyon describes the long struggle.

A correspondent of Erasmus in 1533 sent that scholar a number of selected readings from it, as proof of its superiority to the received Greek text. In 1669 a collation (or statement of its various readings) was made by Bartolocci, but it was never published, and remained unknown until 1819. Other imperfect collations were made about 1720 and 1780. Napoleon carried the manuscript off as a prize of victory to Paris, where it remained till 1815, when the many treasures of which he had despoiled the libraries of the Continent were returned to their respective owners. While at Paris it was studied by Hug, and its great age and supreme importance were first fully known; but after its return to Rome a period of seclusion set in. In 1843 Tischendorf, after waiting for several months, was allowed to see it for six hours. Next year De Muralt was permitted to study it for nine hours. In 1845 the great English scholar Tregelles was allowed indeed to see it but not to copy a word. His pockets were searched before he might open it, and all writing materials were taken away. Two clerics stood beside him and snatched away the volume if he looked too long at any passage! However, the Roman authorities now took the task in hand themselves, and in 1857 and 1859 editions by Cardinal Mai were published, which however, differed so much from one another and were both so inaccurate as to be almost useless. In 1866 Tischendorf once more applied for permission to edit the MS., but with difficulty obtained leave to examine it for the purpose of collating difficult passages. Unfortunately the great scholar so far forgot himself as to copy out twenty pages in full, contrary to the conditions under which he had been allowed access to the MS., and his permission was naturally withdrawn. Renewed entreaty procured him six days' longer study, making in all fourteen days of three hours each; and by making the very most of his time Tischendorf was able in 1867 to publish the most perfect edition of the manuscript which had yet appeared. An improved Roman edition appeared in 1868–81; but the final and decisive publication was reserved for the years 1889–90, when a complete photographic facsimile of the whole MS. made its contents once and for all the common property of all scholars.[2]

The Vatican Manuscript is a rare gem in that it contains in Greek almost all of the Old and New Testaments. The beginning has been lost as far as Genesis 46:28; some of the Psalms are also missing (Psalms 106–138); and the ending likewise has dropped off (Heb. 9:14 to the close, the letters of Timothy, Titus, and Revelation). The General Epistles are included after the Book of Acts, following the usual order of many Greek manuscripts. It is bound in book form (a codex) and embraces 759 leaves of the finest vellum. Each page is about ten inches square and holds three columns of writing which originally were very handsome. The beauty of the handwriting has been marred by some later scribe who thought he could do future generations a great service by tracing over the text whose ink was beginning to fade. The scribe would have performed a greater service if he had left the manuscript alone, for even after more than sixteen hundred years the original ink has not faded from view.

It is distressing that this manuscript is not entirely complete, yet in spite of its gaps it is considered to be the most exact copy of the New Testament known. It is believed to be the earliest of the great uncials, and the many extensive studies, which have proved its text to be of the purest quality, confirm this judgment. The printed texts of the Greek New Testament today rely heavily on the Vatican Codex.

One other point worthy of note concerns the ending of the Gospel of Mark. A fuller discussion of this difficult problem will appear later, but it is sufficient now to observe that the Vatican Manuscript does not include Mark 16:9–20. For some strange reason, however, its scribe left at this point more than a column of space blank in his manuscript. This seems to indicate that he knew of the existence of these questioned verses but was undecided about whether he should include them.

2. The Sinaitic Manuscript (Aleph).[3] Of almost equal importance to the Vatican Manuscript is the Sinaitic Codex. It is known as the Sinaitic Manuscript because it was "discov-

ered" by the great textual critic Constantin Tischendorf at St. Catherine's Monastery on Mount Sinai. The story of this manuscript—how it was found, how it was painstakingly prepared for publication, how it was obtained from the monastery and the controversy that ensued, and how it eventually came to England—is so fascinating that it deserves a chapter all its own. Chapter 4 will relate this story, along with some rather surprising recent events connected with the manuscript.

3. The Alexandrian Manuscript (A). Next in rank among the large vellum uncials is the Alexandrian Manuscript, so called because it is known to have been in Alexandria for several centuries. It was probably brought from Alexandria to

Courtesy of the British Library, London, England

The Sinaitic Manuscript. This page shows the close of Mark's Gospel and the beginning of the Gospel of Luke. In this manuscript the Gospel of Mark concludes with verse 8.

Constantinople by Cyril Lucar who in 1621 became the Greek Patriarch of Constantinople. Cyril and Sir Thomas Roe, the British ambassador at Constantinople, became close allies, and Cyril was obliged to offer the ancient codex to Roe as a gift for James I of England. But James died before the gift could be completed, and so on 1 January 1627 it was presented as a New Year's gift to the new king, Charles I. A part of the Royal Library, the manuscript fortunately survived the disastrous fire of 1731, when the librarian, the famous Dr. Richard Bentley, was seen in his nightgown and great wig, carrying out one of its volumes under his arm. In 1757, with the donation of the Royal Library by George II, it became the property of the newly founded British Museum.[4]

Although at present the Alexandrian Manuscript is bound in four volumes, each bearing the royal arms of Charles I, originally it formed one volume. It contains both Old and New Testaments, mostly complete. Appended at the end of the New Testament are 1 Clement and a portion of so-called 2 Clement. Concerning these additional books, it should be said that 2 Clement is a sermon from the mid–second century. First Clement is a letter presumably written by Clement of Rome about A.D. 95; it is generally classified with the writings known as "the Apostolic Fathers."

But why are these books included in the Alexandrian Manuscript? The question anticipates discussion in chapter 14 on the canon of the New Testament. But in the meantime it is important for Bible students to recognize that in some areas of the church (in Egypt, for example, where Codex A was thought to have been copied), 1 Clement for a while may have had canonical or semicanonical status. Of all the New Testament manuscripts that have come down to us, the Alexandrian Manuscript is the only *Greek* manuscript that includes 1 Clement.

Codex A now comprises 773 leaves: the Old Testament, 630, and the New, 143. Ten leaves are missing from the Old Testament, but the New Testament has suffered more loss (Matt. 1:1–25:6; John 6:50–8:52; 2 Cor. 4:13–12:6). Each page of the manuscript measures approximately 12 1/2 by 10 1/2 inches, with each page containing two columns of writing. Anyone who visits the British Library, or looks closely at photographs of the manuscript, can observe noticeable features that distinguish it from the Vatican and Sinaitic Manuscripts. The form of the handwriting is heavier, certain letters are finished off with added touches (serifs), enlarged letters are used to mark paragraphs, and red ink is used for the first line or lines of each book.

Such features of the manuscript make it possible to date it some time in the fifth century. As for the quality of its text, this varies in different sections of the manuscript. This should not be thought surprising because the various New Testament books at first circulated as single volumes or in combinations of several volumes together, which made it necessary for a scribe to employ several manuscripts in the making of a complete New Testament. Codex A evidences this, for its type of text in Acts, the Epistles, and Revelation is very good (similar to that of the Vatican and Sinaitic Manuscripts), while its text in the Four Gospels is not as good (similar to a form of the text that came to predominate in later manuscripts). These are somewhat technical distinctions, and more will be said later about the nature of variations found in manuscripts.

When the Alexandrian Codex was first presented to the English king, it caused as much excitement at that time as the discovery of the Dead Sea Scrolls has in our day. It was the first of the three great uncials to come to light, and its different readings from correct translations were to usher in a new era of textual investigation.

Summary

Manuscripts of the Greek New Testament fall into two major divisions: uncials and cursives or minuscules. The uncials are those penned in large, capital letters, while the minuscules are those in small letters which often were written cursively. Most of our manuscripts are minuscules, dating from the ninth century. The vellum uncials, some of which date back to the fourth century, are of inestimable worth as witnesses to the

New Testament. The "big three" of the uncials are the Vatican, the Sinaitic, and the Alexandrian Manuscripts. Two of these have become accessible rather recently, and all three have become known since the translation of the King James Bible. Because of its unusual story, I have reserved space in the next chapter for the Sinaitic Manuscript.

For Discussion

1. What is a manuscript? Discuss some of the ways the dates of manuscripts can be determined.
2. Distinguish between uncials and minuscules. Which is the most important group as evidence of the New Testament text? Why?
3. What are the names of the three great vellum uncials? Where is each manuscript located today?
4. Describe briefly some of the main features of the Vatican Codex. How does it rank in importance?
5. Describe briefly some of the main features of the Alexandrian Codex. What is its importance?

The Sinaitic Manuscript

nd the Lord came down upon Mount Sinai, to the top of the mountain; and the Lord called Moses . . . and Moses went up" (Exod. 19:20). According to Exodus 19, Mount Sinai presented an almost indescribable sight—thunders and lightnings, a thick cloud, smoke and fire, the blast of God's trumpet, and the quaking of the mountain. Then, in the hearing of the people, God spoke the Ten Commandments.

For long centuries Jebel Musa, the "mountain of Moses," has been identified as the site where Moses received the Law. Today, below a shoulder of this mountain in a narrow gorge stands impressively the Monastery of St. Catherine. Built by the Emperor Justinian in about A.D. 550, it is one of the oldest of all existing monasteries.

The monastery was built as a fortress—a part of Justinian's rather extensive defense system. But it was also built for the safety of monks in the area who were being raided by Saracen tribes. The monastery was situated illogically in the gorge because the monks pointed to this particular spot as the place where God spoke to Moses in the burning bush (Exod. 3:1–6). Surrounded by high granite walls, the monastery has every appearance of a fort. Inside the walls, the interlacing of narrow passages, covered walks, and whitewashed buildings leave one with the impression of a resurrected Byzantine city.

The monastery bears the name of St. Catherine. Who was Catherine? According to one legend, she was a beautiful, intelligent Christian young lady who refused the immoral advances of the fourth-century Emperor Maximian. She was imprisoned and placed on the wheel to be executed. When the wheel broke, as if it refused her death, she was beheaded. Angels with gentle hands, so the story goes, carried her body to the vicinity of Sinai where, the monks claim, they found it and laid it to rest in the chapel of the monastery.

Through the centuries many pilgrims made their difficult journeys to the monastery. In 1844 a young man of promise came to Sinai at the age of twenty-nine. He came not as a religious pilgrim but as a New Testament scholar in search of the manuscripts at St. Catherine's.

Constantin von Tischendorf

The young man who arrived by camel caravan under the walls of the monastery, who waited for the checking of his credentials and then was hauled over the wall astride a crossbar, was Constantin von Tischendorf. At that time the door was thirty feet high—for protection. Tischendorf, possessed with the special gifts of a quick mind and a brilliant memory, had started his life's work early and was now pursuing it with endless energy. He had resolved to devote himself to the study of the New Testament text and in his words "to reconstruct, if possible, the exact text, as it came from the pen of the sacred writers."[1]

In 1841 Tischendorf had published his first critical edition of the Greek New Testament. At that time, however, textual information from even the most important manuscripts was often defective and from others was not available at all. So Tischendorf proposed to visit the central libraries of Europe in order to copy or collate (make a list of readings) all the uncial manuscripts of the New Testament. Sorely in need of the necessary funds, he was able to scrape together enough to get him to Paris at a time, he says, when he was unable to pay for the suit that he wore.[2]

In Paris, Tischendorf was successful where all previous scholars had failed: he deciphered and published the celebrated Ephraem Manuscript. This extraordinary accomplishment, along with his other publications, enabled him to obtain the means to extend his travels and studies. He visited Holland, England, Switzerland, and Italy, gathering a harvest beyond all his expectations. Then he looked toward the East—to Egypt, to Sinai, to Palestine, to the island of Patmos, to Constantinople, and to Greece. He recorded all these journeys in his *Travels in the East.*

Upon departing on his Eastern venture, he wrote his brother: "Thus I go forth with cheerful confidence. . . . Nor does hope fail me as to the success of my researches with respect to manuscripts. It is thence that Europe has derived its riches, and many a monastery still contains unexamined recesses. . . . Should I never return, I know that I shall have fallen in a worthy cause."[3] It was this "worthy cause" that now brought him to Sinai.

At the monastery Tischendorf was given an apartment of several rooms, including a study, and whatever manuscript he wished from the library. The library itself was in poor condition. Tischendorf entered it with anticipations that had built up for years. After examining the volumes one by one, frequently being disappointed, he then received a great surprise. Tischendorf, twenty years later, tells the story:

It was at the foot of Mount Sinai, in the Convent of St. Catherine, that I discovered the pearl of all my researches. In visiting the library of the monastery, in the month of May, 1844, I perceived in the middle of the great hall a large and wide basket full of old parchments; and the librarian, who was a man of information, told me that two heaps of papers like these, mouldered by time, had already been committed to the flames. What was my surprise to find amid this heap of papers a considerable number of sheets of a copy of the Old Testament in Greek, which seemed to me to be one of the most ancient that I had ever seen. The authorities of the convent allowed me to possess myself of a third of these parchments, or about forty-three sheets, all the more readily as they were destined for the fire. But I could not get them to yield up possession of the remainder. The too lively satisfaction I had displayed had aroused their suspicions as to the value of this manuscript. I transcribed a page of the text of Isaiah and Jeremiah, and enjoined on the monks to take religious care of all such remains which might fall in their way.[4]

In 1845 Tischendorf returned to his home in Leipzig and in the next year published the forty-three sheets he had obtained. They were parts of the Greek Old Testament, the Septuagint. In honor of Frederick Augustus, his patron and the king of his homeland, Saxony, Tischendorf named the work Codex Friderico-Augustanus. Tischendorf continued his labors. In the meantime, however, he told no one where he had found the forty-three sheets. The sheet he had copied from the codex, before he left Sinai, became a goad for him to try to acquire the rest of the manuscript.

So again, in 1853, he came to the monastery at Sinai. How disappointed he was! The whole monastery knew nothing of the precious manuscript he had seen nine years earlier. But he accidentally found a clue to it, a small piece of parchment in the same ancient handwriting of the forty-three leaves, which was being used as a bookmark. The parchment fragment contained a few verses of Genesis 24, proof enough for him that the original codex must have included the entire Old Testament. But at the same time it dawned on him that the bookmark might be all that remained, that perhaps someone else had taken the manuscript away from the monastery. After several more years this seemed even more probable to him. He therefore published the fact that years earlier he had discovered at Sinai not only the forty-three leaves but eighty-six other leaves as well. He wanted the world to know that he had been the discoverer of the ancient manuscript.

In 1859, this time under the patronage of Alexander II, the Czar of Russia, Tischendorf once again made his way to St. Catherine's. Could it be possible that the priceless manuscript was still there, lying undetected in some obscure corner? To the unkempt, disarranged library he went again. He found not a trace of what he was looking for. With these disappointments, now at the age of forty-five, Tischendorf knew he might never return to Sinai.

Tischendorf relates what happened next:

> After having devoted a few days in turning over the manuscripts of the convent, not without alighting here and there on some precious parchment or other, I told my Bedouins, on the 4th of February, to hold themselves in readiness to set out with their dromedaries for Cairo on the 7th, when an entirely fortuitous circumstance carried me at once to the goal of all my desires. On the afternoon of this day I was taking a walk with the steward of the convent in the neighbourhood, and as we returned, towards sunset, he begged me to take some refreshment with him in his cell. Scarcely had he entered the room, when, resuming our former subject of conversation, he said: "And I, too, have read a Septuagint"— i.e., a copy of the Greek translation made by the Seventy. And so saying, he took down from the corner of the room a bulky kind of volume, wrapped up in a red cloth, and laid it before me. I unrolled the cover, and discovered, to my great surprise, not only those very fragments which, fifteen years before, I had taken out of the basket, but also other parts of the Old Testament, the New Testament complete, and, in addition, the Epistle of Barnabas and a part of the Shepherd of Hermas. Full of joy, which this time I had the self-command to conceal from the steward and the rest of the community, I asked, as if in a careless way, for permission to take the manuscript into my sleeping chamber to look over it more at leisure. There by myself I could give way to the transport of joy which I felt. I knew that I held in my hand the most precious Biblical treasure in existence—a document whose age and importance exceeded that of all the manuscripts which I had ever examined during twenty years' study of the subject. I cannot now, I confess, recall all the emotions which I felt in that exciting moment with such a diamond in my possession.[5]

There at last was the fulfillment of his greatest wish. And there was more. Tischendorf had set out to reconstruct the text of the New Testament, using the very best manuscripts at his disposal. Here now was a complete New Testament.

It was about eight o'clock that evening when Tischendorf, with the precious manuscript in his arms, returned to his room in the monastery. Dr. Ludwig Schneller, Tischendorf's son-in-law, has written an interesting biography of Tischendorf in which he says that when Tischendorf reached his room, the first thing he did was to go down on his knees and thank God for the nearly miraculous find.[6]

Tischendorf could not sleep that night. Though the night was cold and his lamp was dim, he sat down and copied out the Epistle of Barnabas. Why Barnabas? Because its full Greek text had been lost for centuries and because it, along with the Shepherd of Hermas, had been regarded as canonical or at least semicanonical in some areas of the church. Early the next morning Tischendorf began to make arrangements that would enable him to copy the entire codex. Within a few days these arrangements were completed, but many negotiations lay ahead concerning the final disposition of the manuscript.

Tischendorf offered generous gifts to the steward who possessed it and for the monastery, but his offers were declined. Having received permission to make a copy of the manuscript, Tischendorf decided that this could best be done in Cairo. One of the monks strenuously objected to this, but the abbot in charge of the monastery, who on business of his own had preceded Tischendorf to Cairo, was the one person who could make the final decision. Because the abbot was intending to travel on to Constantinople, Tischendorf hastened to catch him before he departed. Rushing his caravan across the desert, Tischendorf was able to secure the necessary permission. A Bedouin was then dispatched back to Sinai for the manuscript with the promise of a large "baksheesh" if he speedily carried out his mission. Twelve days later—one can imagine in a cloud of dust—he returned to Cairo with his valuable parcel.

Now the hard work began. With the help of two assistants who knew Greek, 110,000 lines were meticulously copied and checked letter for letter. What proved to be especially challenging were the numerous corrections that had been made in the manuscript. Over the centuries many hands had left their imprints in the form of notes and alterations. Each one of these had to be studiously registered. Working in the stifling heat of a Cairo hotel, Tischendorf and his helpers completed the enormous project in two months.

Yet this was by no means the end. The hastily prepared transcript was insufficient for a truly accurate edition of the manuscript. But a deadlock ensued over Tischendorf's continued use of the manuscript.

Much earlier Tischendorf had hit upon the idea of making the manuscript a gift from the monks to the Russian Czar. But the idea, though favorable at least to some of the monks, could not be acted upon immediately. Eventually, however, Tischendorf was able to secure the manuscript as a gift for the Czar, on the condition that it would be returned if for some reason the proposed gift did not take place.

Tischendorf, with the Czar's approval, proceeded to publish the codex. In doing so, he decided to make an exact reproduction of the manuscript by printing. This meant that new letters had to be made that would closely resemble not only the original handwriting but that of the corrections as well. Every letter, the spaces between the letters, the position and slant of the alterations, the brown and red inks, everything—even the color of the paper used—had to correspond precisely to the original. Yet in two years' time, with all these minutia to attend to, the printing was finished by the spring of 1862. In the fall of that year, three hundred copies of large size were presented to the Czar, who in turn sent out copies as gifts to selected scholars and libraries around the world.

It is sometimes questioned whether Tischendorf acted in good faith with the monks in obtaining the manuscript. In summary, something like the following seems to have taken place. Tischendorf suggested the donation of the manuscript to the Czar, with a hint that the monastery might be handsomely rewarded. The monks seemed at least to agree tacitly but put nothing in writing. The manuscript was loaned with the promise of its return if things did not work out. Tischendorf went ahead to publish the manuscript and dedicate it to the Czar. Negotiations between the disputing monks, on one hand, and the Russian authorities, on the other, dragged on. Finally, an agreement was signed in 1869. The monastery made an official gift of the manuscript to the Czar, and the Czar rewarded the monastery with nine thousand rubles and medals of decoration to various monks. Of course, what actually happened more than a century ago may never be known.[7]

Acclaimed by the world's great universities, Tischendorf has probably been honored more than any other Biblical scholar in history. Although he was very deserving, such honors did not become him. Modesty in these matters was not a virtue he was able to cultivate.

But Tischendorf must be given his due. Why was it that he was able to decipher the Ephraem Manuscript? How was it that he spent years of travel away from home, uncovering unknown manuscripts and rescuing others from oblivion or destruction? Tischendorf himself explains. It was not "mere learned labour" that drove him to his goal. It was rather to "clear up . . . the history of the sacred text" and to recover that text "which is the foundation of our faith."[8]

"Faith" was not a word he was ashamed to use. In fact, his own account of the discovery of the Sinaitic Manuscript is but a preface to his larger pamphlet, *When Were Our Gospels Written?* The pamphlet is a strong statement on the genuineness of the Four Gospels. That is, the pamphlet argues that the Gospels were written by none other than the evangelists whose names they bear. The pamphlet also defends the Christ revealed in these Gospels against those who would "rob the Saviour of his divine character." For "if we are in error in believing in the person of Christ as taught in the gospels, then, the church herself is in error, and must be given up as a deception."[9]

The pamphlet, though originally written in a technical style, was enthusiastically received. The supply of three thousand copies was exhausted in two weeks. A revised and popular version of the pamphlet later circulated widely in several editions and translations.

The Manuscript Today

On prominent display in the British Library (formerly part of the British Museum) is the Sinaitic Manuscript. It first arrived in London on 27 December 1933, purchased from the Russian government by the British Museum for the sum of £100,000 (then a little more than $500,000). More than half of this was donated by the general public. The manuscript came to England by train and with an official delegation to the British Museum by taxi. A large crowd at the museum was awaiting its arrival. When the great manuscript was brought from the taxi, all the men took off their hats.[10]

Of what must have originally comprised about 730 leaves, 393 remain, 245 of the Old Testament and 148 of the New. The leaves are of very fine vellum, measuring approximately fifteen inches square. The text is written four columns to a page, except in the case of seven poetic books of the Old Testament where the text is in only two columns. The handwriting is large and clear, simple yet magnificent.

What about the date of the codex? The style of its script, along with other factors, make it quite certain that it was copied about the middle of the fourth century. It was copied probably by three different scribes; the different spellings of various words make it possible to distinguish between the hands. As noticed earlier, the manuscript includes many corrections, but these are about tiny points that do not materially affect the message of the text.[11]

The Sinaitic Manuscript is the oldest complete manuscript of the New Testament that exists today. This, of course, makes it unique. Its importance, however, lies in the antiquity and quality of its text. Extensive studies have classed it in type with the Vatican Manuscript, which means that the two most important witnesses on the Greek New Testament are the Vatican and the Sinaitic Codices.

Recent Developments

In recent years two developments have taken place concerning the Sinaitic Manuscript that must be mentioned to bring matters up to date. One is an old story with some recent developments; the other is new and rather astounding.

In 1862, when only a few people had seen the manuscript, a Greek named Constantine Simonides burst on the scene with the claim that he had written it in the year of 1840. Experts on the subject considered the claim preposterous, but newspapers vented the controversy. Tischendorf's response was that the claim was "fool's babble" and that years before, in 1856, he had unmasked Simonides as a forger, which had led to his arrest.

Simonides was unable to explain many things. How could he learn the art of calligraphy and copy the entire Old and New Testaments, and this when he was hardly fifteen years old? How could so many pages of a manuscript have faded ink on them, if written so recently? How could he write in different kinds of hands or employ different hands for the corrections?

The recent part of the story is that there is now available a full treatment of this bizarre episode in a work by J. K. Elliott.[12]

The new story on the Sinaitic Manuscript offers the potential of an extraordinary discovery, but information concerning it has been exasperatingly slow to be disclosed. On 26 May 1975 a hoard of manuscripts and art treasures was uncovered at St. Catherine's Monastery. A fire had gutted a certain area, and in the removal of dirt and debris the manuscripts were found. Apparently, more than two hundred years earlier, a ceiling had collapsed and had buried them in the rubble.

It was not until three years later that news of the discovery began to leak out. Information was scanty, and some of the newspaper reports contained inaccuracies. The announcement of the discovery and related data were reported in three articles by Professor James Charlesworth.[13]

More than a dozen leaves missing from the Sinaitic Manuscript have been discovered. These are from the Old Testament, of course, because the New Testament was already complete. In addition, something like four thousand other manuscripts, including fragments, have been recovered. These are by no means all Biblical but are of many types and cover all kinds of subjects. It is reported that most of the manuscripts are in Greek but that many are in other languages.

These newly found manuscripts are the proud possession of the monastery. Although they have been kept in utmost secrecy, they are being prepared for publication by the abbot of the monastery. Who knows what other manuscripts await discovery or full disclosure?

Summary

The wonderful story of the Sinaitic Manuscript—the earliest complete copy of the New Testament known to survive—continues to hold great interest. The initial discovery of the manuscript, a portion of the Greek Old Testament, goes back to 1844, when Tischendorf as a young New Testament scholar first visited the Greek monastery of St. Catherine at Mount Sinai. The later phase of discovery took place in 1859 on Tischendorf's third visit to the monastery. On this occasion he found many more leaves of the Old Testament and the New Testament complete. In time, the manuscript was carefully copied in Cairo and later was presented as a gift to the Russian Czar. After its eventual publication in 1933, the manuscript was purchased by the British Museum. It is now displayed in London at the British Library. Other sheets of the great manuscript, recovered in 1975, await publication.

For Discussion

1. Who was the scholar that discovered the Sinaitic Manuscript? What goal in his life led him to Mount Sinai?
2. Tell about the first discovery of the Sinaitic Manuscript. Why was Tischendorf allowed to take with him only forty-three leaves of the manuscript?
3. What were the circumstances that led to his discovery

of the remainder of the manuscript? Why is this discovery so important?

4. Where is the Sinaitic Manuscript today? How did it happen to be located here?

5. What recent developments have taken place concerning the Sinaitic Manuscript?

5

Other New Testament Manuscripts

othing is more thrilling than for one to look with one's own eyes and to hold with one's own hands some manuscript of the New Testament. The many New Testament manuscripts are scattered all over the world. In Europe and Asia large collections are deposited in the great national libraries and museums, in the prominent universities, in the many libraries of monasteries and cathedrals, and in the special acquisitions of private collectors. In America most of the large university libraries, especially in the Eastern section of the country, house some of these Biblical treasures. You may go to such centers of learning as Harvard, Princeton, Duke, and Chicago, ask the curator for the privilege of seeing some manuscripts, and there gain a firsthand acquaintance with the materials which have preserved for us our Bible.

We have learned that the most important manuscripts are those of the uncial group. The three outstanding uncials, the Vatican, the Sinaitic, and the Alexandrian, provide in the main the foundation for our New Testament books. This is not to leave the impression that all other manuscripts and witnesses are of little value. Indeed, without the many other textual authorities we could not evaluate properly these three great uncials.

Two Fifth-Century Uncials

After devoting a special chapter to the sensational discovery of the Sinaitic Manuscript, it is time to turn our attention to some of the other manuscripts of the New Testament. To the list of the three grand uncials, we now add two other well-known New Testament witnesses.

4. The Codex of Ephraem (C). At different times materials used in writing were difficult to obtain. This was often the case in the Middle Ages. One way to overcome this shortage was to take an old parchment, wash or scrape off the ink, and then use the scraped-off parchment as if it were new. This kind of manuscript is known technically as a *palimpsest,* a Greek term that has passed into English and literally means "scraped again." Not a few old parchments like this have come down to us, some having been used several times.

In the case of a palimpsest or rescript (rewritten) codex, often the old writing was imperfectly rubbed out; and when a new text was written over the old one, enough remained so that the old text could be seen underneath. Certain chemical reagents could be applied to bring out the older layer of writing. (Ultraviolet photography and computer-enhanced images are now used.) Thus many valuable texts have been recovered from palimpsests.

The Codex of Ephraem is an outstanding palimpsest manuscript with an interesting historical background. As originally written, the Codex of Ephraem was a manuscript of both Old and New Testaments, but for some reason many of its leaves were torn off and lost. In about the twelfth century, someone took the remaining leaves and copied thirty-eight sermons of Ephraem of Syria over the Biblical text. (This was by no means the only time when sermons have covered up the Scripture text!)[1] The Codex of Ephraem thus takes its name from the top layer of writing. The manuscript had been in Paris since the 1500s, and attention had been called to the earlier layer of writing. Yet no one, except in parts and imperfectly, had been successful in transcribing the text underneath.

In 1840 Tischendorf, at the age of twenty-five, came to Paris to attempt the Herculean task of deciphering the palimpsest. When the young scholar asked for the codex, he was greeted with smiling skepticism. Nevertheless, full of hope, he began to pore over the manuscript. The work was extremely slow. The faint, washed-out ink had to be examined letter by letter. Finally, with the aid of chemical reagents, Tischendorf attained his goal, issuing the New Testament portion in 1843, the Old Testament portion in 1845. His unusually fine eyesight and unrelenting perseverance allowed him to triumph where others had failed.[2]

The Biblical text of the codex is not complete. Much is missing from the Old Testament, but for the New Testament there are 145 leaves from every book except 2 Thessalonians and 2 John. The writing, though only one column to a page, in other respects resembles that of the Alexandrian Manuscript. Dating back to the fifth century, the Codex of Ephraem is a very important manuscript, yet the quality of its text does not measure up to the high standard of the fourth-century uncials.

5. The Codex Bezae (D). In the restricted manuscripts area, stored away in a metal cabinet, Codex Bezae is the prized possession of the Cambridge University Library. It derives its name from the Protestant reformer, Theodore Beza, who after having it for more than twenty years, presented it in 1581 to the library at Cambridge University. The manuscript contains (with gaps) the Four Gospels, Acts, and a fragment of 3 John in Latin. Its leaves are somewhat smaller than the manuscripts described so far, measuring ten by eight inches. In all, the codex presently consists of 406 leaves of thin vellum and is now bound in two volumes of convenient size.[3]

Codex Bezae is in many ways a different kind of manuscript. It is the earliest example of a bilingual manuscript; that is, it is written in two languages, with the Greek text on the left side of the page and the Latin text on the right. The lines, written one column to a page, are "sense lines." This means that the lines vary in length and correspond to pauses required as the codex is being read. The Gospels appear in the so-called Western order: Matthew, John, Luke, and Mark.

Because of its distinctive readings, Codex Bezae has the dubious distinction of being the most curious of all the early manuscripts. Its additions and omissions at times put it in a class by itself. Beza himself looked with suspicion upon his manuscript, as did many of his contemporaries. At the time the King James Version was made, Codex Bezae was the only important uncial available; but it was little used because of the speculation that surrounded it.

Due to its unique character, many studies have been done on Codex Bezae. Again and again it departs from the established text. Luke 9:55 adds the words, "And he said, 'You do not know of what spirit you are.'" Luke 23:53, speaking of Jesus' burial by Joseph of Arimathea, says that "he placed over the tomb a stone which twenty men could scarcely roll." Acts 12:10 relates that when Peter and the angel came out of prison, "they descended the seven steps." Acts 19:9, as it tells of Paul's discussions in the lecture hall of Tyrannus, adds the time of day, "from the fifth to the tenth hour." Acts 28:31 concludes the Book of Acts with the additional statement "that this is Jesus the Son of God, through whom the whole world will be judged."

These are only a few examples. Nevertheless, they illustrate that Codex Bezae often has differences from the usual text that involve not just verbal changes but additional clauses and even sentences. What accounts for such differences? The many proposed solutions have not resulted in a satisfactory answer.

Codex Bezae and a few other textual witnesses are the chief representatives of a type of text that is commonly called "Western." This is an early form of the text, examples of which have been found in various geographical areas. Generally speaking, the Western text is characterized by fondness of paraphrase, textual expansions, and striking omissions.

To the student who meets these textual variations for the first time, this may be confusing. If, however, such differences present a problem, we must recognize that these same differences help in providing an answer to the problem. For instance, in Luke's account of the Lord's Prayer, in the middle of the verse (11:2), Codex Bezae adds, "Do not babble on as the others; for some think that they will be heard for their many words. But when you pray . . ." Although this is almost a verbatim quote from Matthew 6:7, Bezae is the only manuscript that has it in Luke. Similarly, Bezae's reference to the stone "which twenty men could scarcely roll" in Luke 23:53 has no other textual support, except from one Old Latin manuscript and the Sahidic (an Egyptian) Version.

So as one examines a large number of Western variants, one comes to suspect that they are secondary and do not belong to the text as originally written. On the other hand, this does not mean Bezae should be simply cast aside. It is a very valuable manuscript, but it must be used wisely. It dates back to about the fifth century; and though it includes such variants as those already mentioned, in large measure it preserves the Gospels and Acts as they always have been known. In other words, we should not forget that Bezae has far more agreements with the Vatican and Sinaitic Manuscripts than disagreements. These numerous agreements, especially when confirmed by other types of witnesses, make the text as certain as it can be.

Other Uncials

Having made reference to a "Western" kind of text in Codex Bezae, we should pause here to give further explanation. New Testament manuscripts, depending on their similarities, are generally divided into three groups or types of text: Alexandrian, Western, and Byzantine. The latter, associated with the Byzantine world of the Middle Ages, is the type of text found in the vast majority of the later manuscripts. The Alexandrian text, connected with Alexandria in Egypt and represented especially by the Vatican and the Sinaitic Manuscripts, is very early and is regarded as the best form of the text.

Other uncials can be treated more briefly. Altogether about 280 uncials are now listed.[4]

Codex Claromontanus (D^p or D_2), so designated because it came from Clermont, France, is a sixth-century manuscript of Paul's letters (including Hebrews). It is a small volume of

533 leaves, written on thin vellum. In certain respects it is similar to Codex Bezae. It once belonged to Theodore Beza, it is written in both Greek and Latin, and its text type is Western. Edited by Tischendorf, it is located at the National Library of Paris.

Codex Laudianus (E^a) takes its name from Archbishop Laud, who presented it to the Bodleian Library at Oxford in 1636. Dated at the end of the sixth century, written in Greek and Latin, it contains the Book of Acts (with omissions at the end). Although it has Western characteristics, its Greek text is mostly in agreement with the Byzantine form of text. It is the earliest manuscript that includes the eunuch's confession in Acts 8:37.

Codex Regius (L) is an eighth-century codex of the Gospels, now in the National Library in Paris. It preserves a good, Alexandrian type of text, often agreeing with the Vatican Manuscript. At the end of Mark, it includes the traditional ending (Mark 16:9–20) and also a shorter ending. But the shorter ending is supported by only three other Greek manuscripts and a few witnesses among the versions, all of which (except one) include the longer ending as well.

The Freer Washington Manuscripts were obtained in 1906 by Mr. Charles L. Freer of Detroit. One manuscript (Codex I) contains a collection of Paul's letters from 1 Corinthians through Hebrews, with Hebrews being placed after 2 Thessalonians. The text is Alexandrian in type, dating back to the fifth century; but, unfortunately, less than half of the manuscript has survived. The other manuscript (Codex W) is a copy of the Four Gospels, dating from the fourth or fifth century. Its type of text may be best described as a mixture, probably indicating that it was copied from portions of several manuscripts. Both Freer manuscripts are located in the Freer Gallery of Art, the Smithsonian Institute, Washington, D.C.

Minuscule Manuscripts

Brief notice should be made concerning the minuscules. They date from the ninth century and comprise the vast majority of the manuscripts that exist today. While the list of known manuscripts is still growing, at present there are about 2,800 minuscules. By and large, they represent, along with many later uncials, a later form of the text (Byzantine).

Listed below are a few of the small-letter manuscripts that are important either from a textual or historical standpoint.

Minuscules 1 and 2 are Gospels manuscripts of the twelfth century which are now located in Basle, Switzerland. These minuscules head the list because they were used by Erasmus, who edited the first Greek New Testament. Erasmus mainly used minuscule 2, which is a Byzantine-type manuscript.[5]

Minuscule 13 is a twelfth- or thirteenth-century manuscript in Paris. It is one of about a dozen manuscripts that comprise "Family 13," especially unique for its location of the adulterous woman passage not in John 7:53–8:11 but after Luke 21:38.

Minuscule 33, of the ninth century and in Paris, contains the Gospels, Acts, and Epistles. Because of its good text, it has long been called "the Queen of the Cursives."

Minuscule 61, of the fifteenth or sixteenth century and in Dublin, Ireland, was the first manuscript found in support of the Three Heavenly Witnesses passage in 1 John 5:7–8. On the authority of this manuscript alone, Erasmus added 1 John 5:7 to the third edition of his Greek text.

Minuscule 565 is a copy of the Gospels from the ninth century, located in St. Petersburg, Russia. It is a beautiful codex, an outstanding example of a number of manuscripts written in gold or silver letters on purple vellum.

Minuscule 1739 is a tenth-century manuscript of Acts and the Epistles, located in one of the many monasteries on Mount Athos in Greece. It is a significant manuscript because its ancestor apparently goes back to the fourth century, having a text similar to the Vatican Manuscript.

The above lists of uncials and minuscules are necessarily short, but perhaps they are enough to quicken the reader's interest in the many manuscripts that have conveyed the New Testament message down through the centuries.

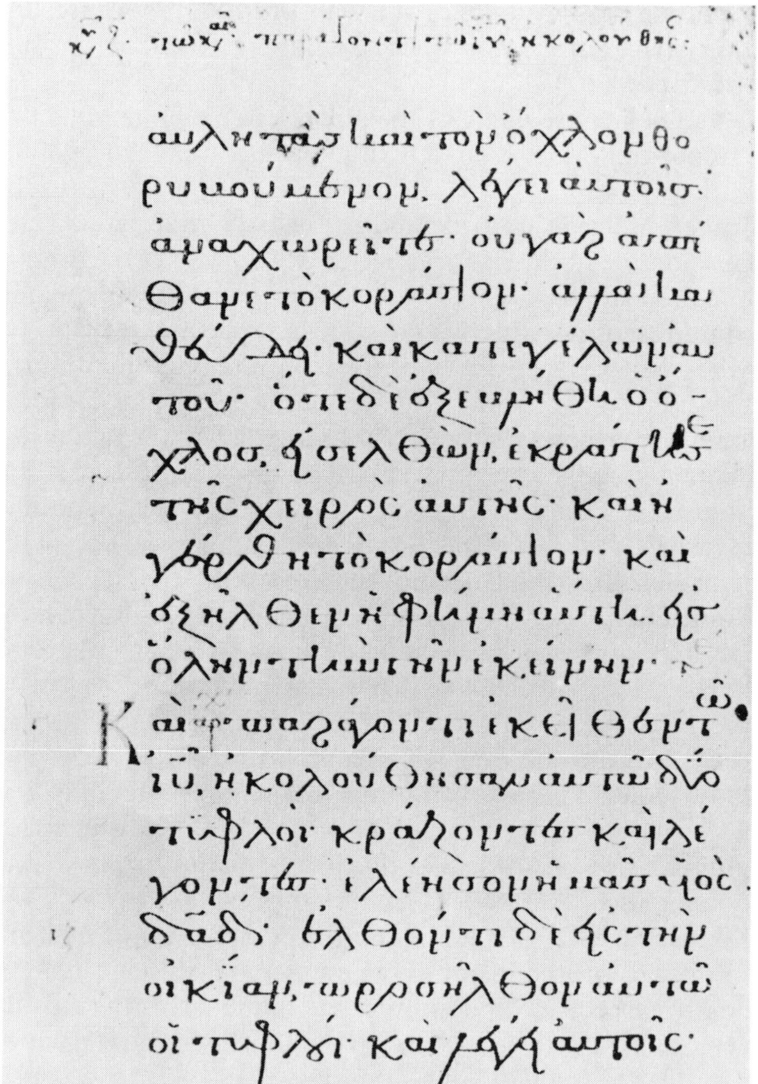

A typical late minuscule manuscript of the New Testament.

The Lectionaries

One further word needs to be added concerning New Testament manuscripts. Included in their number is a group of materials known as "lectionaries." The term "lection" refers to a selected passage of Scripture designed to be read in public worship services, and thus a lectionary is a manuscript especially arranged in sections for this purpose. Most lectionaries are of the Gospels, but some are of Acts and the Epistles. Lectionaries cannot be classified as uncials or minuscules because there are extant copies of both types. Studies have shown that lectionaries, being intended especially for public worship, were copied a little more carefully than ordinary manuscripts. But much work yet needs to be done on the lectionary texts. More than 2,200 lectionaries have been enumerated.[6]

There is still another group of manuscripts that did not become known until recent times. These manuscripts are those that were written on papyrus—our earliest copies of the text of the New Testament. We will postpone until later an account of their discoveries and their significance for the Biblical text.

Summary

In this chapter two other manuscripts have been added to the list of the outstanding uncials. Altogether this makes five vellum uncials that are dated in the fourth and fifth centuries: the Vatican, the Sinaitic, the Alexandrian, the Ephraem palimpsest manuscript, and Codex Bezae. Of these, the first two in particular, the Vatican and the Sinaitic, with the help of other witnesses, supply the textual foundation for the New Testament. But other uncials and the minuscule manuscripts add much support. On the basis of common characteristics, New Testament manuscripts may be classified generally in three groups or types of text: Alexandrian, Western, and Byzantine. The Western text, because of its suspicious variations, and the Byzantine text, because of its later date, cannot measure up to the superior quality of the Alexandrian type of text. The Alexandrian is regarded as the best form of the text.

For Discussion

1. What are the two fifth-century manuscripts added in this chapter to the list of important uncials? Which of these is a palimpsest manuscript? What is a palimpsest?
2. Why is one manuscript called the Codex of Ephraem? How is the name of Tischendorf associated with it?
3. Why is the other manuscript known as the Codex Bezae? How is it different from many other manuscripts?
4. What is a lectionary? What are the approximate dates for (1) the uncial manuscripts and (2) the minuscules?
5. What are the three groups into which New Testament manuscripts can be divided? Which of these is regarded as being the best form of the text?

6

Ancient Versions:
The New Testament

p to this point we have been examining the primary sources for the New Testament text. We come now to consider the early versions or translations. As we proceed, however, we should keep in mind that the versions, because they are translations, are necessarily secondary in rank as witnesses to the text. Something is always lost by way of translation.

The gospel that needed proclamation in different tongues on the day of Pentecost was the same gospel which, when written, demanded translation into other languages. After the apostolic messages began to circulate in Greek among early Christians, the next step was to circulate these same messages in other tongues. Wherever Greek was unknown or unnatural, translations from Greek into the native languages began to spring up. Of these, three were very early and are of chief importance: the Syriac, the Latin, and the Coptic (Egyptian). The Syriac and the Latin versions date certainly back into the second century, and the Coptic probably goes back almost as far. Of course, we do not possess Latin or Syriac copies that early, but it is possible with our existing manuscripts to trace the kind of text in use at that time. Thus the ancient versions open to us an entirely independent line of evidence on the New Testament text.

The Syriac Versions

Syriac was the main language spoken in the regions of Syria and Mesopotamia and is almost identical to Aramaic. It was undoubtedly one of the earliest translations to be made; it could be used not only by the Jews who did not know Greek but also by the natives of Mesopotamia, where the gospel may have entered in the last part of the first century.

1. The Diatessaron. Perhaps the earliest form of the Syriac version is what is known as the *Diatessaron*. The Greek term means "through four," meaning "through the Four Gospels," and refers to a harmony arrangement of the Gospels. Tatian, a native of Mesopotamia, lived in Rome for many years, where he was converted to Christianity by reading the Bible. He became a pupil of Justin Martyr; after the martyrdom of Justin, Tatian returned to his home near the year A.D. 170. At about this time he compiled his harmony by merging the Four Gospels into one continuous account of the life of Christ. Whether this was done at Rome or in Syria is not known, nor is it known whether Tatian composed his harmony in Greek or Syriac. But it is known that Tatian's harmony circulated widely and was so popular that special measures had to be taken in the fifth century to remove it from use in Syrian churches.

The Diatessaron then fell into oblivion. No copy of it remains, and its text must be imperfectly constructed on the basis of secondary sources.[1] Yet one or two sidelights on the Diatessaron may be of interest.

In the middle of the nineteenth century, much controversy was being stirred up by certain German scholars who maintained that the Gospels could not have been written earlier than about A.D. 140. In support of this view some even questioned whether there was ever such a thing as the Diatessaron. On the other hand, its existence would show that the Four Gospels were generally accepted no later than the third quarter of the second century, and thus must have been written much earlier. If the disputants in the controversy had only known! Already in print was an Armenian translation of the commentary of Ephraem, written in the fourth century, which was based on the Diatessaron. This in itself would have put an end to the controversy about the existence of the Diatessaron. Clearly, there can be no question about its existence and that it was constructed out of our four canonical Gospels.

Of interest also is another bit of information on the Diatessaron. On the banks of the Euphrates, at Dura-Europas, the Romans had built a fortress which was captured by the Persians in A.D. 256. Excavations there uncovered a number of papyrus and vellum fragments. One of the vellum fragments, identified in 1933, contains a few lines of the Diatessaron in Greek. The remarkable discovery did not prove that Tatian originally wrote his harmony in Greek, but it does demonstrate that a Greek Diatessaron was in use even in this remote corner of Syria not many years after its composition.

2. The Old Syriac. Only in the nineteenth century did it become known that there was such an early translation as the Old Syriac. It may be that it predates the Diatessaron, but this is not the general consensus.

There are two chief manuscripts of the Old Syriac: the Curetonian Syriac and the Sinaitic Syriac. The Curetonian Syriac is a fifth-century copy of the Gospels, consisting of over eighty leaves. It is so called because of the labors of Dr. William Cureton. In 1842 the British Museum obtained a large number of Syriac manuscripts that had come from one of the monasteries in the desert west of Cairo. In 1848 Dr. Cureton, a keeper of manuscripts in the museum, demonstrated that the text of this manuscript is of an earlier type than the common Syriac.

The Sinaitic Manuscript was discovered in 1892 by widowed twin sisters, Mrs. Agnes Smith Lewis and Mrs. Margaret Dunlop Gibson. These Cambridge ladies—wealthy, eccentric, and intellectual—came to St. Catherine's Monastery at Sinai in quest of rare Biblical manuscripts.[2] Here Tischendorf made his astounding discovery, and here other important manuscripts were to be uncovered. In pursuit of their goal, the twins examined a number of manuscripts, one of which was an old palimpsest document. The layer underneath was identified by Mrs.

Lewis as a Syriac copy of the Gospels, and subsequent studies have shown it to be a representative of the Old Syriac translation. In fact, it is the earliest known copy of the Old Syriac, reaching back to the fifth or possibly to the fourth century.

The form of text found in the Old Syriac is mixed in character, containing Alexandrian type readings but more often those that are "Western." Interestingly, the Curetonian Syriac includes Mark 16:9–20, but the Sinaitic Syriac does not have it.

3. The Peshitta. The word *Peshitta* means "simple" and refers to the standard Syriac translation which has been in use since the fifth century. It is a revision of the Old Syriac, based on Greek manuscripts that attest to an early form of the Byzantine-type text. There are more than 350 manuscripts of the Peshitta, but the testimony of these is not as fundamental as that of the Old Syriac.

The Coptic Versions

Coptic was the latest phase of development of the ancient Egyptian language, which eventually came to be written in Greek characters. A number of Coptic dialects exist, but two are especially noteworthy.

The Sahidic Version is written in the dialect of Upper (Southern) Egypt, whose main city was Thebes. The Sahidic formerly was known primarily from fragments; but in the twentieth century extensive manuscripts have come to light, dating to the third and fourth centuries.

The Bohairic Version refers to the dialect in Lower (Northern) Egypt, in areas near Alexandria and in the delta region. The Sahidic seems to be earlier than the Bohairic; the latter, however, has some manuscripts that go back to the fourth and fifth centuries.

But why single out these two versions in particular? The answer lies in the good quality of their texts. The gospel of Christ made quick inroads into Egypt, and fortunately Egypt has preserved an early form of the text. The Sahidic and Bohairic often confirm this type of text—the same type of text found in such as the Vatican and Sinaitic Manuscripts.

The Latin Versions

The remainder of this chapter will be given to the Latin versions. These versions should hold special interest for all English-speaking people because the first translation of the English Bible was made from the Latin.

The Old Latin

In A.D. 180 persecution broke out against the church in Numidia of North Africa. There, in a small town named Scillium, Christians were arrested, put on trial, and then decapitated in nearby Carthage. The record of their court trial survives. Speratus, one of the Christians, was asked what he had in the chest he carried with him. He replied, "Books and letters of Paul a just man."[3]

The books to which Speratus referred were undoubtedly translations in Latin, for it is not likely that the people in Scillium knew Greek. So by this time the Epistles of Paul existed in Latin; and if Paul's letters were in Latin, surely the Gospels had been translated into Latin as well.

The Latin of these translations is what we now know as Old Latin. Why, where, and when did it have its origin?

You will recall that the various books of the New Testament were all written in Greek. When in the A.D. 50s Paul wrote his letter to the Romans, he wrote in Greek. Other writers either writing to or from Rome likewise used Greek as late as the mid–second century and beyond.

In time, however, Rome would need its Bible in Latin as well; this may have happened about the same time Latin versions appeared in Africa. The time was as early as A.D. 160 or before, and perhaps earlier for books of the Old Testament.

In a similar way, Latin translations came into use in other areas of the Empire. At first they were probably made informally by missionaries or by local Christians to assist congregations in their worship. So it seems that the first Latin translations arose independently, differing from one another. More and more copies were made, and the eventual result was a number of variant readings among the Latin manuscripts.

The Latin Vulgate

These differences in the Latin texts set the stage for a series of events that would culminate in the translation of the Latin Vulgate. If we are to understand more about the Vulgate, we must learn more about the person who produced it.

1. Jerome. Eusebius Hieronymus, known as Jerome, was born about the year 345 at Strido(n) in Dalmatia (an area northwest of modern Greece). When he was about twelve, his well-to-do parents sent him to Rome, where he studied advanced Latin grammar, Greek, and the Latin classics. Later, his higher education concentrated on rhetoric, designed for the career of a lawyer or civil servant.[4]

During these years Jerome had been only nominally Christian; after leaving Rome, he committed himself to the life of an ascetic. Yet one thing he could not give up: his love of classical (pagan) literature.

At Antioch, he was attacked with a severe fever and was near death. One of his letters relates what happened.[5] In a dream he was caught up before "the Judge's judgment seat" and was asked to state his condition. He replied that he was a Christian. But the divine response was, "You lie; you are a Ciceronian, not a Christian."

For Jerome, the dream was a shattering experience. He resolved to devote the rest of his life to the study of the Scriptures. Following the dream, he was off to the sun-drenched desert to live among the Syrian hermits. In the desert for four or five years, he had much time for study. Here, under the guidance of a converted Jew, he began to learn Hebrew.

When, therefore, in 382–83, Bishop Damasus of Rome saw the need of drawing together the various Old Latin translations into one official edition, who was more qualified for the task than Jerome? By now Jerome had returned to Rome and was serving Damasus as his secretary and translator.

Damasus' commission to revise the Old Latin must have given Jerome joy mixed with pain. On one hand he recognized the importance of his task, on the other he could foresee how unfavorably it might be received. In 384 Jerome finished his revision of the Four Gospels. Dedicating his preface to Damasus, he writes:

> You urge me to revise the Old Latin version. . . . The labor is one of love, but at the same time both perilous and presumptuous. . . . Is there a man, learned or unlearned, who will not, when he takes the volume in his hands, and perceives that what he reads does not suit his settled tastes, break out immediately into violent language and call me a forger and a profane person for having had the audacity to add anything to the ancient books, or to make any changes or corrections therein.[6]

We are not sure whether Jerome revised the rest of the New Testament.[7] At any rate, his stay in Rome was cut short. Damasus died in 384, which left Jerome without the prestige he once enjoyed. Besides, many Roman Christians were opposed to the ascetic ideal that Jerome defended. So much resistance had built up against him, he was forced to leave Rome.

In the company of his friends, Jerome journeyed to the Holy Land and took up residence in Bethlehem. Here he was able to continue his work on the Latin Bible and complete the Old Testament.

How was his work on the New Testament received? Shortly after he finished his revision of the Gospels, he had to defend himself. He did not suppose that "any of the Lord's words [were] . . . in need of correction" or that any of them were less than "divinely inspired." His only purpose was to restore the Latin manuscripts to conform to the original Greek. Of his detractors he said, with characteristic sarcasm, "If they dis-like water drawn from the clear spring, let them drink of the muddy streamlet."[8]

Following his work on the Old Testament, he spent his last years writing Biblical commentaries, pamphlets, and letters. Always he was in the center of controversy, as a churchman intent on devouring heretics, as a monk arguing for and over-stating the Scriptures on marriage and virginity, or as a scholar contending ardently for his views. In all he was a man of great strengths and of great weaknesses.

But Jerome is remembered today for his labor on the Latin Vulgate. It was to remain his crowning achievement.

2. After Jerome. Thus far we have referred several times to the Latin Vulgate. The Latin term *vulgata* means "common" or "commonly accepted." In Jerome's time *vulgata* applied either to the Old Latin Version or to the Septuagint (the Greek transla-tion of the Old Testament)—both were "commonly accepted." In other words, until Jerome's revision successfully displaced the Old Latin, it would not be known as the Vulgate.

It was not until 1546 at the Council of Trent that Jerome's version officially received the title "Vulgate." But it had been generally received long before this. The process began slowly, but by the sixth and seventh centuries Jerome's version had mostly won the victory over the Old Latin.

Of course, as time passed and the number of copies increased, Jerome's Vulgate itself went through various revisions. One of these revisions is of particular interest. In the thirteenth cen-tury in Paris, the need arose for a Bible that could be more easily used. Probably at this time Stephen Langton, a leading theologian at the University of Paris, arranged the Vulgate into the modern chapter divisions still in use today.

Value of the Latin Versions

As we conclude, we should state in summary form the value of these translations.

1. The Old Latin was the first to be made in the Latin tongue, important for Latin-speaking Christians and important wherever they carried the gospel. As for its kind of text, the Old Latin is typically "Western."

2. The Vulgate now numbers 10,000 or more manuscripts. It has been copied more than any other book in the Christian era. Historically speaking, it ranks next to the Septuagint as the most important translation ever made.

3. The Vulgate New Testament was not based on the Greek. It was Jerome's assignment to revise the existing Old Latin, but thankfully he did check the Greek manuscripts. We do not know what these manuscripts were, but in the Gospels, for example, he seems to rely mainly on a text similar to that of the Vatican and Sinaitic Manuscripts.

4. The Vulgate reigned as the Bible of Western Europe for a thousand years. When at the end of the Middle Ages demand for the knowledge of Scripture increased dramatically, it was the Vulgate that was first translated into the languages of the people.

5. The Vulgate was the first book of importance to be printed. About 1450 Johann Gutenberg of Mainz, Germany, perfected the use of movable type. In 1456 the "Gutenberg Bible" was issued. It was a beautiful Latin Bible, whose appearance marked a new epoch.

6. The Vulgate for English-speaking people remains of special interest. Many words used in English translations are due to the Latin Vulgate. A short list of such terms includes "congregation," "consecration," "conversion," "exhortation," "justification," "ministry," "sanctification," "testament," even "Olivet" and "Calvary."

7. Eventually the Vulgate was made the official Bible of the Roman Catholic Church, and so it remains today. The result is that the Roman Catholic Bible in English is a translation of a translation and is not a translation from the original languages.

Summary

In addition to the Greek manuscripts, much information is available to us from the ancient translations. Three of these are especially important: the Syriac, the Latin, and the Coptic. The Coptic versions, in particular the Sahidic and Bohairic, exhibit a good quality type of text that was current in Egypt early in the Christian era. Tatian's harmony of the Gospels, known as the Diatessaron, may be the earliest form of the text in Syriac, but no manuscript of it has survived. Otherwise, the main Syriac versions are the Old Syriac and the Peshitta, the latter being represented in more manuscripts while the former is the more important as a witness to the text. It was Jerome who gave us the Latin Vulgate, which has had an incalculable influence on Western civilization. In the West the Latin Vulgate was the standard Bible for a thousand years.

For Discussion

1. Why is the evidence of the ancient versions important? Is their witness to the New Testament primary or secondary? Why?
2. In connection with the Syriac versions, identify the following: (1) Diatessaron, (2) Agnes Smith Lewis, and (3) Peshitta.
3. What are the Coptic versions? What bearing do they have on the New Testament text?
4. What are some of the highlights of Jerome's life? What was his commission from Damasus?
5. Why is Jerome's translation called "the Latin Vulgate"? Why should we learn about it? What is the Vulgate's significance for English-speaking people?

Manuscripts of Special Interest

he previous chapter surveyed the earliest and most important versions of the New Testament: the Syriac, the Coptic, and the Latin. Of these, the Latin versions, and especially Jerome's Vulgate, have had a pervasive influence on all of Western civilization. In the East the Scriptures circulated in Greek, Syriac, Coptic, Armenian, Georgian, and other languages; in the West they were copied in Latin alone. During the Middle Ages most books were written in Latin. Latin was the language of communication among nations. Latin was the language of monasteries, the centers of learning for much of Europe. Latin was the language of the educated man, whether he lived in Italy, France, Spain, or England. This explains why so many copies of the Vulgate exist today and also why so many of the vernacular translations owe their origins to the Latin.

This chapter directs attention to several manuscripts that are of unique interest. Here, as throughout our study, we have to be selective. Some of these manuscripts may not be familiar to many people, but they are illustrious and must be included in any catalog of great manuscripts.

Aids to Readers

In order to appreciate these wonderful manuscripts, we will need to learn more about some of the special features typically found in medieval manuscripts.

A reader of a medieval manuscript could avail himself of many kinds of helps. A New Testament manuscript would include traditional titles for each book and often notes at the end of the book. These endnotes usually state where a book was written or by whom it was written or sent. The King James Version includes these notes at the end of each of Paul's letters. It should be emphasized, however, that these are only traditional notes and often cannot be relied upon.

Likewise, each book of the New Testament was divided into chapters but not verses. Yet the chapters were entirely different from those in our modern Bibles. The system found in most of the manuscripts had many chapters: sixty-eight in Matthew, forty-eight in Mark, eighty-three in Luke, and so on. Each chapter was given a title, such as "About the Blind Man." A list of the chapters was drawn up and placed before the book.

Other material often included introductions to the various books, accounts of the lives of the Four Evangelists (Matthew, Mark, Luke, and John), of the life of Paul, and so forth. Notes or comments on the meaning of the text are in the margins, just as we might write notes in our Bibles today. In the past extensive commentaries by churchmen were handed down; these commentaries fill the margins and surround the text in many manuscripts.

Of special interest are the "Eusebian Canons." Eusebius, known as "the Father of Church History," who lived in Palestine in the fourth century, was somehow responsible for a system of locating parallel passages in the Gospels. In addition to the previously mentioned chapter divisions, the Gospels were further divided into smaller sections. These sections were numbered, and the number for each section was written in the margin. All the sections were listed to show which section was parallel to which in Ten Tables, or Ten Canons, which were placed before the Book of Matthew.

The Eusebian Canons represented an ingenious tool by which similar material in the Gospels could be consulted and studied. They became nearly indispensable for a Gospels manuscript, and in the Middle Ages they were a beautiful, decorative feature of manuscripts.

Illuminated Manuscripts

The subject of beautifully adorned canons leads to that of illuminated manuscripts.[1] "Illumination" is a term applied to the decoration of books or manuscripts with colors or gold or silver. "Miniature" is the word for a picture in an illuminated manuscript. Derived from a term meaning "red paint" (Latin, *minium*), "miniature" did not come to its current meaning until modern times.

The earliest Biblical texts are plain in appearance. Gradually, however, touches of decoration were added to the manuscripts, at first to mark the separation of the several books that were copied in one volume. Then came the addition of color for headings and large initials embellished with nearly every form of bird, animal, fish, monster, human being, and angel.

Portraits of the Evangelists are the chief decoration found in many manuscripts. Each portrait covers a full page and may be found at the beginning of each Gospel or joined all together at the beginning of the codex. The Evangelists are usually pictured as seated, copying their Gospels, with writing instruments on a table close at hand. In Greek manuscripts the Apostles Matthew and John are represented as old men with gray hair and beards, while Mark and Luke are rendered as younger.

In Latin manuscripts, however, there are marked differences. The Evangelists may be represented as old or young, with or without beards. But one feature in Latin manuscripts stands out especially: the symbols of the Evangelists. The symbols are characteristic of Latin art, for no Greek manuscript employs them unless it is extremely late.

From early times Christians had associated the Four Evangelists with the "four living creatures" of Ezekiel and Revelation (Ezek. 1:5–10; Rev. 4:6–7). Ezekiel describes the four living creatures as having the form of men, each with four faces and each with four wings. The four faces are those of a man, a lion, an ox, and an eagle. For some unknown reason, the forms of these faces, in the order presented by Ezekiel, came to stand for the Four Evangelists: a man for Matthew, a lion for Mark, an ox or calf for Luke, and an eagle for John, each represented with wings.[2]

Special Manuscripts

Sumptuous, deluxe editions of the Scriptures were produced. These were inscribed in gold or silver on vellum dyed a brilliant purple, the special color of the imperial rank. Roman emperors possessed such splendid manuscripts of classical texts. In Constantinople—"new Rome," as it was called—the art of writing on purple leaves continued and from there extended to other areas. A number of these sumptuous manuscripts have survived, at least in part.

Extraordinarily beautiful copies of other manuscripts have likewise survived. Three of these are Latin manuscripts of particular interest. One is the most valuable witness on the text of the Vulgate. The other two are grand, indeed, often described as the most beautiful books in the world. It so happens that all three originated in the British Isles.

In the last years of the sixth century, Augustine and his fellow monks came to southeast England as missionaries, using the visual aids of a silver cross and a painting of Christ on a wooden board. Within a few years the mission was well established in Canterbury and had received from Rome a number of books. Some of the books presumably included illuminated manuscripts, whose pictures could be used by missionaries in their evangelism.

In addition to those received in Canterbury, large numbers of books came to northern England. This brings us to the story of the famous Codex Amiatinus. It is the earliest complete Vulgate copy of the Bible known, and it is also the best manuscript of the Vulgate.

Benedict Biscop, who by about 680 had founded twin monasteries at Wearmouth and Jarrow in northeast England, made frequent trips to Italy. On these journeys he brought back books of all kinds, which he deposited in the monasteries. These, along with other additions, provided a rich supply from which the monks could copy their own books.

Amiatinus was copied at Wearmouth/Jarrow. It was one of three large Latin Bibles made under the direction of Ceolfrid, a monk who had succeeded Benedict at his death. Of the three Bibles, Amiatinus is the only one that has survived.

Ceolfrid had intended it to be a gift for the pope, sent, as reads the note inside, "from the farthest ends of England." In 715 Ceolfrid and his companions set out on their journey to carry the manuscript to Rome, but Ceolfrid died on the way. Whether the Bible reached Rome is not known; but what is known is that for centuries it belonged to the monastery of Monte Amiata, thus the name Codex Amiatinus.

Amiatinus is a huge volume and weighs about seventy-five pounds. It has 1,040 leaves, accurately copied in a beautiful hand. Today it is located in the grand Laurentian Library at Florence.

The two other manuscripts to be considered here are the Lindisfarne Gospels and the Book of Kells. Incomparable in their colors and designs, they are truly masterpieces of art in manuscript.

More than 150 years before Augustine's arrival in England, Patrick and others brought the message of Christ to Ireland. There the monks were able to master the craft of ornamental design in manuscripts. From Ireland the art of manuscript illumination was exported to the island of Iona, off the west coast of Scotland. As an offshoot of Iona, a monastery was established at Lindisfarne, a small island near the coast of northeast England. Here the Lindisfarne Gospels were written, as a later note in the manuscript says, "for God and St. Cuthbert."[3]

Cuthbert had joined the community of Lindisfarne and gained in his lifetime a reputation for saintliness. In 698, eleven years after his death, his bones were dug up and reverently buried. It is almost certain that during this time the beautiful Lindisfarne Gospels was copied, illuminated, and put on display.

The adversities of this manuscript illustrate the chance survival of many manuscripts. In 793 Lindisfarne was sacked by Viking pirates. After successive raids on other monasteries, in

875 the remnant of monks fled Lindisfarne, taking with them Cuthbert's body and their Gospels manuscript. During an attempt to cross over to Ireland, a storm arose and swept the manuscript overboard. Shortly afterward the monks, walking along the shore, joyfully found their manuscript unharmed. Subsequently, Sir Robert Cotton acquired the manuscript for his superb book collection, which eventually passed on to the British Museum.

Examination of the Lindisfarne Gospels reveals its extraordinary worth. Its main text is a good quality copy of the Latin Vulgate. Its subordinate text, made two and a half centuries later, is an Anglo-Saxon translation made word-for-word between the lines of the Latin. The translation is of special interest to English-speaking people because it represents the oldest extant version of the Four Gospels in any form of English.

The illuminations in the Lindisfarne Gospels are a marvel. They include fifteen full-page decorations, sixteen pages of arcades for the Eusebian Canons (see page 81), and numerous decorated initials throughout the codex. But what is striking about the illuminations is their endless details—multiple geometric patterns, spiral and trumpet forms, bird and animal shapes and more—all executed in a variety of colors.

Two illustrations may be chosen to demonstrate the wonder of the manuscript. In one of these the Evangelist Matthew appears with a halo and his book in hand (see page 82). Above him is his symbol, blowing a trumpet. To the right is a haloed figure with a book, partially visible behind a curtain. This may represent Christ (cf. Heb. 6:19–20), perhaps indicating the ultimate source of Matthew's Gospel.

Another illustration is of the large initial page that begins Luke's Gospel (see page 83). On the left is a Q, the first letter of the Latin text, filled in with an amazing combination of patterns. On the right is a catlike figure, stretched out to form a border. The illuminator used red dots for backgrounds and designs. On this one sheet more than ten thousand red dots have been counted!

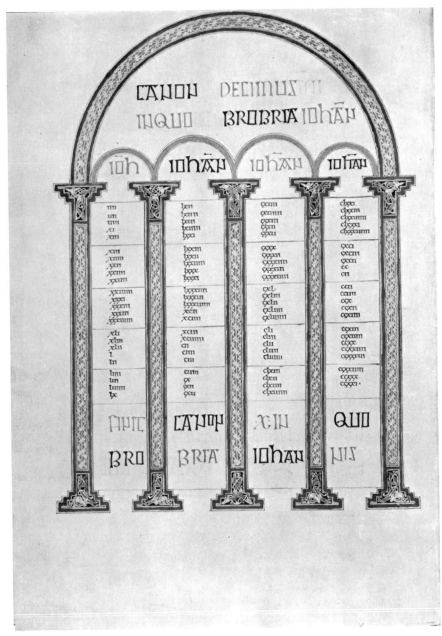

The Lindisfarne Gospels, the last page of arcades for the Eusebian Canons.

(81)

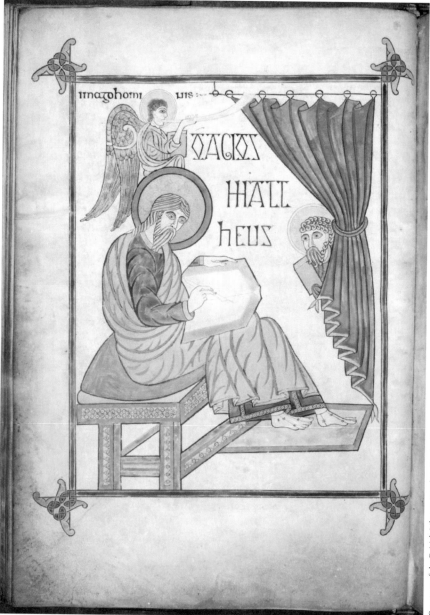

The Lindisfarne Gospels, full-page representation of Matthew.

The Lindisfarne Gospels, initial page of the Gospel of Luke.

One other manuscript must be mentioned—the famous Book of Kells. In the world of books, many scholars rank it as the greatest wonder of the world.

Both the date and place of origin of this celebrated manuscript remain uncertain. Its date is probably about A.D. 800 or earlier. As for its origin, the best guess is that it was produced in Iona by Irish monks who escaped to Ireland in 806 after Viking raids had killed most of them. The survivors settled at Kells, near Dublin, bringing with them their precious manuscript.

It is generally acknowledged that in variety and complexity of design, the Book of Kells towers above all manuscripts of its class. A traveler to Ireland tells of a wonderful manuscript which he saw about the year of 1185.

> This book contains the harmony of the four Evangelists according to Jerome. . . . Fine craftsmanship is all about you, but you might not notice it. Look more keenly at it, and you will penetrate to the very shrine of art. You will make out intricacies, so delicate and subtle, so exact and compact, so full of knots and links, with colours so fresh and vivid, that you might say that all of this was the work of an angel, and not of a man.[4]

This may indeed be a description of the Book of Kells. Kells was known to be the home of the manuscript from the eleventh or twelfth century and perhaps much earlier.

Today the Book of Kells is proudly exhibited in the library of Trinity College, Dublin, where it has been since the seventeenth century. It is a large manuscript of the Four Gospels, written in a beautiful Latin script. The manuscript contains 680 pages and is now bound in four volumes. Trinity College displays two volumes at a time, the volumes and pages being changed regularly.

Although its text is important, what astonishes visitors as they crowd around the famous manuscript is the lavish decoration of the text. Full-page illuminations abound. A full page is devoted to each of the Four Evangelists, to each of their symbols, to Christ and scenes of his life, to the beginning of each Gospel, and so forth.

Every page of the manuscript is decorated, except two. Initial letters are ornamented in a vast assortment of colors and shapes. Men, dragons, lions, cats, or birds may fill the shape of an initial or be seen walking between the lines of the text. The variety of the patterns is immense, made by use of compasses. Indeed, the whole work is so complex that it must have been executed by a master group of scribes and artists. One can scarcely imagine the patient labor and excellent eyesight required for such an accomplishment.

What conclusions can be reached about such dazzling decorations of manuscripts? First, they supplied the reader with visual helps for a large manuscript that did not have modern chapter and verse divisions. Second, they offered the reader graphic illustrations of the text and the gospel in pictures to the person who was unable to read. Third, by magnificent adornment of the text, they bestowed honor on the revealed Word of God.[5]

In spite of our interest in the artistic appearance of these manuscripts, the most important thing about them is their beautifully written text of Scripture. Of course, Codex Amiatinus, the Lindisfarne Gospels, and the Book of Kells are only samples of what was being produced in the early medieval period. Extend these kinds of works through the centuries, to the East and to the West, and one can begin to envision the great number of manuscripts made in many languages during the thousand years of the Middle Ages. Even though a host of these manuscripts are irrecoverably lost, we are fortunate that thousands remain.

Summary

Long before the use of modern chapters and verses, medieval manuscripts included many helps for readers. Divisions of the text into small units, traditional titles for each book, endnotes, the Eusebian Canons, comments on the text—such material is typically found in manuscripts of the Middle Ages. An "illuminated" manuscript refers to a manuscript lit up with color decorations. Portraits of the Four Evangelists frequently adorn the pages of medieval manuscripts. The Latin manuscripts in particular often include the Four Evangelists with their symbols. Codex Amiatinus, the Lindisfarne Gospels, and the Book of Kells are examples of magnificent manuscripts that have survived. Amiatinus is a complete Latin Bible with an excellent text of the Vulgate. The Lindisfarne Gospels and the Book of Kells are wonderful manuscripts that may well deserve to be known as the most beautiful books in the world.

For Discussion

1. What aids were available for the reader of a medieval manuscript? What advantages did they offer? What were some of their disadvantages?
2. What is an "illuminated" manuscript? What is a "miniature"? Describe the miniatures of the Four Evangelists and their symbols.
3. What is the origin of Codex Amiatinus? Why is it important to learn about this manuscript?
4. Why is the Lindisfarne Gospels so named? Where is it located today? Beyond its artistic beauty, why should it be especially interesting for English-speaking people?
5. Why is the Book of Kells so named? Where is it located today? Why do you think it continues to attract many visitors?
6. Jerome was one among many who condemned the making of luxuriant manuscripts. Would you agree or disagree with Jerome? Why?

The Text of the New Testament

e have learned that the original autographs of the New Testament are no longer in existence. We may wonder why the Supreme Governor of the world would allow this to happen. We may be tempted to ask why God did not in some way collect all of the original books of the inspired writers and store them up through the years for safekeeping. Final answers to these questions cannot be given by humans. Nevertheless, we can see that if the written record was to be spread, some copies had to be made from the originals. We also can see that as more and more copies were made, it was but natural for new copies to replace the timeworn originals.

Yet problems arise and persist in the making of books. In modern books it is not unusual to see glaring mistakes. Some of the greatest mistakes in the history of the Bible have occurred since the invention of printing. More than four hundred errors in the first edition of the King James Bible were corrected in a subsequent edition two years later.[1] In our own time, despite all concentrated efforts to the contrary, translations such as the Revised Standard Version and the New International Version have not been exempt from the plague of misprints.

If in modern times errors somehow appear in printed copies of the Bible, it is not difficult to see how mistakes slipped unnoticed into the New Testament manuscripts long ago. All ancient books had to be produced by hand, and no human hand is so exact or eye so sharp as to preclude the possibility of error. So errors were made, errors were copied, and errors were mixed in with the pure text.

Textual Criticism

The presence of these errors in the text of the Bible has given rise to a highly advanced science known as textual criticism. This science is also referred to as lower criticism, in contrast to higher criticism. While higher criticism devotes itself to such things as the study of authorship, date of composition, and historical value of a given Biblical document, lower criticism is concerned only with the form of words—the text.

The function of the textual critic is plain. He seeks by comparison and study of the available evidence to recover the exact words of the author's original composition. The New Testament text critic seeks, in short, to weed out the chaff of bad readings from the genuine Greek text. He realizes that his task is as important as the message which is borne in the text. He also realizes that if the Greek text is faulty, all translations from the Greek will likewise be at fault.

Mistakes of Copyists

It is possible to look back over existing manuscripts and classify the types of mistakes made by the ancient scribe. Manuscript faults come about in two ways. Either the alterations made by the scribe are unintentional slips or else the alterations are made deliberately.

1. Unintentional errors. Mistakes of the hand, eye, and ear are of frequent occurrence in manuscripts but usually pose no problem because they are so easy to pick out. Often a scribe with a copy before him mistakes one word for another and so by chance writes down the wrong word. Sometimes a scribe

confuses words of similar sound, as in English we often inter-change "affect" and "effect."

A few New Testament passages may serve as illustrations. In Romans 5:1, is it "let us have peace with God" or "we have peace with God"? The difference is simply whether the *o* in Greek is long or short (*echōmen* or *echomen*). In 1 Thessalonians 2:7, is it "we were babes among you" or "we were gentle among you"? The difference is one letter (*nepioi* or *epioi*). In 1 John 1:4, is it "that your joy may be full" or "that our joy may be full"? The difference between "your" (*hymōn*) and "our" (*hēmōn*) is one letter and the two words sound alike. In Revelation 1:5, is it "washed us from our sins" or "freed us from our sins"? The difference is one letter and the words sound the same (*lousanti* or *lusanti*). It is not difficult to see how these scribal mistakes could take place. Generally, if they are important enough, our recent translations will footnote such differences to ensure the reader is well informed.

Errors of omission and addition are common in all the manuscripts. Words sometimes are omitted by a copyist for no apparent reason, simply an unintentional omission. More often, however, omissions are due to the similar appearance of words at a corresponding point several lines above or below in the manuscript. The scribe's eye might skip, for example, from the end of line 6 to a similar word at the end of line 10. A scribe might add to his copy in the same way. He may inad-vertently transcribe a word twice in succession, or repeat a letter twice, or write a letter once when it should be written twice. Not a few times the scribe may misunderstand the pas-sage due to improper division of the words, especially if the scribe is unskilled in the language. When this happens, we can sympathize with the scribe, remembering that during most of the uncial period the style of writing was to crowd the letters together in such a way as to leave the words without interven-ing spaces between them. But in all matters of this kind, the textual critic, by comparison of the many manuscripts, can detect and explain these errors without hesitation.

Another form of error, more difficult to solve, grows out of the practice of writing explanatory notes in the margin. These marginal notes are somehow incorporated in the main body of material and thus become a part of the text. But it should be stressed that the New Testament manuscripts rarely exhibit this kind of error, and that when it does occur, our many textual witnesses keep us on the right course.

2. Intentional errors. Unintentional alterations in the manuscripts are many, but the vast majority of them are of little consequence. What presents a more serious problem to the textual critic are the variant readings that have been purposefully inserted by the scribe. We ought not think these insertions were made by dishonest scribes who simply wanted to tamper with the text. Almost always the intention of the scribe is good and he wants only to "correct" what appears to be an error in the text. So if a word seems improperly spelled, or a Greek verb does not have the proper ending, or a form does not correspond with the classical idiom, then the scribe feels it is his duty to improve the text he is copying.

Again, citing one or two examples may illustrate the point. In John 7:39 the text literally reads, "for not yet was the Spirit." Because this could be taken to mean that the Spirit was not in existence at that time, some manuscripts and versions add the word "given" for the phrase to read, "the Spirit was not yet given." To further clarify, a large number of manuscripts supply "holy," that is, "Holy Spirit." In a similar way, the word "church" *(ekklesia)* is added in Acts 2:47 in the later manuscripts to clarify a rather obscure Greek expression *(epi to auto)*. In these cases the scribes, with all good intentions, mistakenly thought that their additions were necessary in order to bring about a better understanding of the text.

A scribe especially might try to remove any difficulty in the texts of the Gospels. If he found a statement of Jesus in one Gospel similar to a statement in another, he might modify one to make it in perfect agreement with the other. This may explain a variant found in two verses of Matthew and Luke. The King James Version of Matthew 11:19 reads, "But wisdom is justified of her children," an exact parallel of Luke 7:25. However, the more recent translations of Matthew have "works" instead of "children" in agreement with our earliest manuscript authorities. We surmise that at some early date "works" was changed to "children" by a copyist to bring the phrase in harmony with Luke's Gospel. Thus we are practically certain that originally the two records of Jesus' sayings were not the same. This, to be sure, is what one frequently finds in the Gospels, for in quoting Jesus, the Gospel writers often do not give his words verbatim.

Basic Rules of Textual Criticism

The above textual variation ("children" or "works") can be explained in other ways as well. Over a period of several centuries, textual criticism has formulated a number of fundamental rules, called "canons of criticism," which have proved to be inestimably valuable in deciding between variations in manuscripts. These rules are not hard and fast but only serve as general principles to guide and stabilize the textual critic.

With the above problem in mind, it is interesting to see what happens when some of the leading principles of textual criticism are followed. One basic rule is that the more difficult reading is to be preferred. At face value, without further explanation, this rule may be misleading. Obviously, some scribal errors of omission or addition scramble up the text to the extent of nonsense. When this is the case, if the more difficult reading is to be preferred, the text would be meaningless. Ruling out blunders of this kind, practically always the more difficult reading will prove to be the better reading. This is true because it was a natural tendency for the scribe to simplify the text that he was copying.

Keeping this principle in mind, which reading is to be preferred in Matthew 11:19—"children" or "works"? Which of the two is the more difficult reading? Undoubtedly the more difficult reading is "works," which leaves a difference of one word between Matthew and Luke.

Solving this question of one word in Matthew also serves to illustrate other important textual principles. In any given problem the *quality* of witnesses to the text is much more important than the *quantity*. Or, as it is often put, textual authorities must be weighed rather than counted. Thousands of manuscripts and versions may support a certain reading; but if they are of late date and stand opposed to the early uncials, their witness should be rejected. In the case of Matthew 11:19, what is the evidence from the manuscripts and versions? And where shall we go to find such information?

We shall attempt to answer the latter question briefly and then proceed to our original inquiry. If you are reading Matthew 11:19 in the Revised Standard Version, you will see a footnote that reads, "Many ancient authorities read *children:* as in Luke 7:35." (The New Revised Standard Version has the same note but omits the reference in Luke.) This note is sufficient for most people; but if you are interested in reading exactly how the ancient authorities read, you will need to go to a recent edition of the Greek New Testament. Here you will find at the bottom of the page a series of abbreviations, generally referred to as an "apparatus," which indicates the textual authorities for and against "works" in Matthew 11:19.[2]

What is the textual evidence on "children" and "works"? In favor of "children" are the Ephraem Manuscript and Codex Bezae (both from the fifth century) and almost all of the other later manuscripts as well as the Old Syriac and the Latin versions. Against "children" and in support of "works" are the Vatican and Sinaitic Manuscripts (both from the fourth century) and a few other witnesses. This means there are literally thousands of copies of manuscripts and versions that read "children" and only a handful that read "works." Nevertheless, the *quality* is in support of "works," as found in the Vatican and Sinaitic Manuscripts. Because of the agreement of these two early uncials, along with other factors, all of the recent translations read "works" in Matthew 11:19. Very often, as here, if the Vatican and Sinaitic Manuscripts support a particular reading, this is sufficient authority for the reading. This well illustrates the unchallenged supremacy that these two uncials sustain as witnesses on the New Testament text.

Still another important rule enters in here. In parallel texts, as we find in the Gospels, *different* readings are usually preferred. All of the Gospels present but one view of Jesus, that he is the Son of God. Yet in presenting this view their individual descriptions of him and his sayings often employ different words. Through the years, these verbal distinctions, either intentionally or unintentionally, tended to be "harmonized" by the scribes. Thus it is a sound conclusion that in parallel accounts the text which preserves minute verbal differences is generally the better text. In our example of Matthew 11:19, the earliest manuscripts retain a verbal distinction between the two accounts. This is an added reason for believing that "works" is the preferable reading.

Of course, textual criticism has many other rules, some of which are much more technical in character. Hopefully these few examples provide something of an insight into the mind of the textual critic. What an unexperienced person might consider a maze of bewildering information on a given text, a trained specialist will regard as a wealth of material in which has been preserved the original reading.[3]

Summary

The New Testament books have been handed down to us by means of thousands of copies. Although God inspired the New Testament writers, he did not miraculously guide the hands of the copyists. Textual criticism seeks to counteract inevitable scribal errors and recover the true form of the text. Many mistakes in the manuscripts crept into the text unintentionally and are not difficult to detect. Other textual modifications were made intentionally, usually by well-meaning scribes, and these do not stand out so clearly. Yet even in these cases a textual critic is equipped with a multitude of aids to overcome the problem. In a case like Matthew 11:19, "works" is a better reading than "children" because (1) the quality of witnesses is more important than the quantity, (2) the more difficult reading is to be preferred, and (3) the different reading in parallel passages is usually the more reliable one. These are a few illustrations of the many sound principles upon which textual criticism is based. Because textual criticism is a sound science, our text is secure and the textual foundation of our faith remains unshakable.

For Discussion

1. What is the task of textual criticism? Is it to be identified with lower or higher criticism?
2. What are some ways in which unintentional mistakes may be made in manuscripts? What are some examples of intentional variations? Of the two groups, which presents the more difficult problem for the textual critic?
3. What are some of the basic rules of textual criticism?
4. How is it possible that the authority of a few manuscripts can outweigh the testimony of many witnesses? What could be the result if this rule were not followed?

9

Significance of Textual Variations

t is a fact that the New Testament text has been transmitted to us through the hands of copyists. It is also a fact that, since these hands were human, they were susceptible to the slips and faults of all human hands. It is not true, therefore, that God has guided the many different scribes in their tasks of copying the Sacred Scriptures. The Scriptures, although divine, have been handed down through the centuries by means of copies, just like any other ancient book. A failure to recognize this would mean that God would have to perform a miracle every time a scribe picked up pen and ink. And this assumption is almost inconceivable!

Number of Variations

Suppose someone were to say there are 200,000 errors in the New Testament text. What would be our response? And if 200,000 errors are in the text, how can we be sure that we have the original New Testament message?

From one point of view it may be said there are 200,000 scribal errors in the manuscripts. Indeed, the number may well considerably exceed this and obviously will grow as more and more manuscripts become known.[1] But it is wholly misleading and untrue to say that there are 200,000 errors in

(95)

the text of the New Testament. (Actually, the word "error" is consciously avoided by textual critics; they prefer to speak of "textual variants.") This large number is gained by counting all the variations in all of the manuscripts (above 5,300). For example, if one slight variant were to occur in 4,000 different manuscripts, this would amount to 4,000 "errors." But this is how one can arrive at the large number of 200,000 "errors." A person is either unlearned or of a skeptical mind who tries to take this large number of variations and use it in such a way as to undermine one's faith in the Word of God.

In this connection one fact especially needs to be emphasized. This large number of variations exists in exact proportion to the number of manuscripts that we possess. There are far more copies of the New Testament than of any other book from the ancient world. Because we have more New Testament manuscripts, we have more variations. Suppose we had only ten manuscripts of the New Testament. In so few manuscripts the total number of variations would be small. But if we had only ten manuscripts, the New Testament text would not stand on as sound a ground as it otherwise does. *If the large number of manuscripts increases the total of variations, at the same time it supplies the means of checking them.*

Consequences of Variations

What about the significance of these variations? Are these variations immaterial or are they important? What bearing do they have on the New Testament message and on faith? To respond to these questions, it will be helpful to introduce three types of textual variations, classified in relation to their significance for our present New Testament text.

1. Trivial variations which are of no consequence to the text. The great majority of variant readings in the manuscripts have to do with trivial matters, many of them so minute that they cannot be represented in translation.

Perhaps the best way to demonstrate this is to open at random a page of the Greek text. Let us take the same page that was consulted previously in order to learn the evidence pro and con for the reading "works" in Matthew 11:19. On this small page fourteen verses (Matt. 11:10–23) appear. A quick look at the bottom of the page shows that nine variant readings are listed.[2] At first glance nine variants out of fourteen verses seem alarming. Yet every other variant on the page, besides "children" or "works," is trivial in nature. Several of the variants concern the omission or addition of such words as "for," "and," and "the"; others have to do simply with different forms of the same or similar Greek words. In one case the variant concerns the omission or addition of the verb "to hear" (whether to read "the one who has ears" or "the one who has ears to hear"). At no point is there a real problem of the text, except with the alternative of "children" or "works," which as we have seen is rather easily resolved.

This page of variants is typical of the mistakes found in our copies. Very often words in the Greek copies are spelled slightly differently over a period of years. This becomes especially noticeable with vowels that sound alike, the interchange of *e* and *i*, *ei* and *i*, *ai* and *e*, and so forth. Of course, such adjustments are not surprising, especially when we recall how much English words have changed their spelling during the last few centuries. One has only to take in hand a copy of the first edition of the King James Bible of 1611, and one will quickly see what a great change a few centuries have made on the form of English words. These changes have occurred since the printing press supposedly standardized the English language. In a similar way the Greek language was undergoing change, and the natural thing for the scribe to do was to alter his copy in keeping with the accepted standards of his day. Variations in grammar and even vocabulary are to be explained on the same basis.

Other examples may be cited. Proper names often presented problems to the scribes. In Acts 18:24, is it "Apollos" or "Apelles" or "Apollonios"?[3] In John 1:28, is it "Bethabara beyond the Jordan" or "Bethany beyond the Jordan"? In John 5:2, is the name of the pool "Bethzatha" or "Bethesda" or "Bethsaida"? Likewise, a variation may be no more than a change in the order of words. In Matthew 1:18, is it "the birth of Jesus Christ" or "the birth of Christ Jesus"? (Other manuscripts have "the birth of Jesus," while others read "the birth of Christ.") In all of the above cases, the manuscripts read differently; but the variants are so minor that they are scarcely referred to in the footnotes of our translations.

Examples like these can be found numerous times. Yet in all these cases we have an abundance of information that enables us, even in trivial matters, to make a concrete decision as to the likely reading of the original text. And even if we did not have this information, if we were left completely in the dark with reference to such things as spelling, word order, and other comparative minutia, still we would not be in danger of losing the Divine Revelation.

2. Substantial variations which are of no consequence to the text. We do not wish to leave the impression that all textual variants can be lightly dismissed. Some variations involve not only a word or two but a whole verse or even several verses. Certainly variations of this kind are more than trivial. It should be hastily added, however, that these variations of a substantial character do not affect our present text. They do not affect our text today because they are not supported by the most authoritative textual witnesses.

A few examples will clarify what we mean. Codex Bezae of the fifth century has already been discussed in chapter 5. This manuscript often has peculiar readings, one of which is found after Luke 6:4. Here it transfers verse 5 after verse 10 and inserts the following: "On the same day, seeing one working on the sabbath day, he said to him, 'Man, if you know what you are doing, you are blessed; but if you do not know, you are accursed and a transgressor of the law.'" This curious incident is recorded in no other manuscript or version. It is beyond doubt a substantial variation, but we are sure that it was not a part of Luke's original Gospel. It in no way changes our text because modern textual criticism has unhesitatingly rejected it.

A more familiar passage found in our early English translations illustrates the same principle. The story of the adulterous woman (John 7:53–8:11) involves a number of verses and clearly represents a substantial variation. Almost all recent translations by varying devices mark this account as textually uncertain. The American Standard Version, the Revised Standard Version, the New Revised Standard Version, and the New International Version either separate it from the text or include it in brackets. The New English Bible and the Revised English Bible place it at the close of John's Gospel. The translations briefly explain to their readers the reasons for their actions.

Why have these later translations looked with suspicion on these verses? The answer is simple: no early manuscript, except one, and practically none of the early versions have the story of the adulterous woman in them. The one early manuscript which contains the story is the very one (Codex Bezae) that is known for its peculiar readings, as we have seen above in the case of Luke 6:5. Otherwise, it is necessary to come down to manuscripts of the eighth century and later before the story is found again. In addition, some of the manuscripts that have it also have notes of doubt in the margin concerning it; others put it at the end of the Gospel of John; and still others insert it in the Gospel of Luke, after Luke 21:38. Certainly, there were grave doubts all along concerning this passage.

But do these past doubts place our text in a questionable atmosphere? Certainly they do not. Just as we accept the reading "works" instead of "children" (Matt. 11:19) on the evidence of the early manuscripts, so here on the basis of the early manuscripts we do not include the adulterous woman story in our text. Where did the story come from? No one knows, but it was probably a tradition handed down from the primitive church. Our early manuscripts do not deny the truthfulness of the story but attest that it was not an original part of John's Gospel. Nor do the vast majority of scholars question the authenticity of the incident. The statement of the respected F. J. A. Hort may be taken as typical: "the story itself has justly seemed to vouch for its own substantial truth . . ."[4]

Another passage of interest is found in Acts 8:37. The King James translation of this verse reads, "And Philip said, if thou believest with all thine heart, thou mayest. And he answered and said, I believe that Jesus Christ is the Son of God." These words are represented as part of a conversation between Philip the Evangelist and the eunuch at the time of the eunuch's baptism. These are familiar words, stressing the importance of faith in Jesus Christ. Yet the words are not found in the American Standard Version or the Revised Standard Version. These and other recent translations, on the basis of the evidence, are compelled to omit this verse from the Book of Acts. It is true that a sixth-century uncial, some good minuscule manuscripts, and the Old Latin Version support the verse, but practically all the other manuscripts and versions stand opposed to it. Because no Greek manuscript earlier than the sixth century knows of this reading, beyond doubt it could not have formed a part of the original account of Acts.

The case of 1 John 5:7 is less complex. The King James Version reads, "For there are three that bear record in heaven, the Father, the Word, and the Holy Ghost: and these three are one." An interesting circumstance led to the introduction of this verse in the English Bible. After the invention of printing, the first person to publish an edition of the printed Greek text was a Dutch scholar by the name of Erasmus. His first edition came out in the year 1516. But the first and second editions of Erasmus did not include 1 John 5:7. A mild controversy was stirred up because the verse was indisputably in the late Latin copies. Erasmus insisted that his text was right and was so sure of himself that he rashly promised to include the verse in his text if one single Greek copy could be found in support of it. At length a copy turned up, and Erasmus, true to his word, included the verse in the third edition of his Greek Testament. William Tyndale was the first man to translate the New Testament into English based on a Greek text (instead of Latin); and it was Erasmus' third edition that he employed in making his translation. So from Tyndale down to the King James Bible, 1 John 5:7 has been a part of English Scripture.

The textual evidence is against 1 John 5:7. Of all the Greek manuscripts, only two contain it. These two manuscripts are of very late dates, one from the fourteenth or fifteenth century and the other from the sixteenth century. Two other manuscripts have the verse written in the margin. All four manuscripts show evidence that this verse was apparently translated from a late form of the Latin Vulgate.

These are examples of significant variations, but actually they do not have a bearing on our text today. They do not affect our text simply because there is not enough evidence for them to have an effect. Thus the American Standard Version, which habitually makes explanations when its text varies from the King James, does not so much as note 1 John 5:7 in its margin and instead rearranges the verse structure. First John 5:7, Acts 8:37, and John 7:53–8:11 reflect substantial variations in some manuscripts; but since they are unknown in the early uncials, they cannot cast doubt on our improved text today.

3. Substantial variations that have bearing on the text. It remains now to consider a group of textual readings which at some points raises questions about our text. It would be a simple task to ignore these things. But facts are facts, and our ignorance of them solves no problems.

Of interest to all, and a passage that well illustrates textual variations which affect our text, are the twelve verses at the end of Mark's Gospel. In practically all recent English translations, these last verses are separated from the main body of the text. Some translations also give an alternative "shorter ending" of Mark. But since this ending is supported by only a few manuscripts and versions and certainly seems to have been written several centuries after the time of Mark, one wonders why it should be included at all.

The problem of Mark 16 is rather unique. In the cases of 1 John 5:7, Acts 8:37, and John 7:53–8:11, there really is no problem because all the authoritative evidence looks in one direction. But this is not the case with Mark 16—the evidence apparently looks in two directions. The evidence against Mark 16:9–20 mostly rests on the Vatican and Sinaitic Manuscripts. These two uncials of the fourth century are our very best manuscripts and as textual witnesses are acknowledged as being in a class by themselves. We are thus confronted with the problem that the two manuscripts which we rely upon most do not have these closing verses of Mark. Additional significant evidence is against Mark 16:9–20, including the witness of the earliest known manuscript of the Old Syriac, the earliest known manuscript of the Latin Vulgate, a large number of Armenian manuscripts, and so forth.[5]

Other factors are against the acceptance of Mark 16:9–20. Although it is difficult to argue on the basis of vocabulary, nevertheless about twenty terms and expressions do not fit in with Mark's style of writing. Some of these expressions never occur (1) in the rest of Mark or (2) elsewhere in the Four Gospels or (3) anywhere else in the entire New Testament. Further, verses 8 and 9 do not seem to connect well, changing from the subject of the women disciples (v. 8) to Jesus' post-resurrection appearances (v. 9). And is it not strange that Mary Magdalene is "introduced" to the reader in verse 9 even though she has been present from verse 1?

But in favor of Mark 16:9–20 are a host of witnesses: the Alexandrian Manuscript, the Ephraem Manuscript, Codex Bezae, other early uncials, all late uncials and minuscules, a number of Old Latin authorities plus the Vulgate, one old Syriac manuscript, the Syriac Peshitta version, and many other versions. Besides, there is a plain statement from Irenaeus, an early Christian writer, which clearly shows the existence of Mark 16:9–20 in the second century and the belief that Mark was its author.

In brief, this is the negative and positive data on the question. On one hand is the unparalleled reliability of the Vatican and the Sinaitic Manuscripts; on the other hand is almost all of the other manuscript evidence. J. W. McGarvey wrote a capable defense of Mark 16:9–20 in his *Commentary on Matthew and Mark*. It was published, however, in 1875, before the great work of Westcott and Hort on the Greek text was completed. Yet McGarvey's position, with a few minor modifications, can stand with credit today. But the problem persists: What about the negative evidence of the Vatican and Sinaitic Manuscripts? Is it best to say simply that the last leaf of Mark's Gospel may have been accidentally torn away?

Whatever the correct view, it is important to note that the truthfulness of this passage is not in dispute. The main events of Mark 16:9–20 are recorded elsewhere, so at any rate we are not in danger of forfeiting heavenly treasure. The variant readings in the manuscripts are not of such a nature that they threaten to overthrow our faith. Except for a few instances, we have an unquestioned text; and even then not one principle of faith or command of the Lord is involved. Further assurances concerning our text will follow.

Summary

A large number of variations do exist in the manuscripts, but this number is ascertained by counting all the variants in all the manuscripts. When this is understood, the large figure of textual differences does not seem frightening. Most variations are made up of minute details, either obvious scribal blunders or slight changes in spelling, grammar, and word order. These are of no consequence to our text. Other variations might have considerable weight on our text, but they are not supported by the early textual authorities. A few variations present problems for our text, but they are not impossible to solve. Even if they were, since the number of them is so few, these should not be stumbling blocks to our faith.

For Discussion

1. How would you explain a large number (200,000) of variations in the New Testament manuscripts? How is this large number derived?
2. What are some examples of trivial variations?
3. Why do recent translations of the Bible not include (1) the story of the adulterous woman, (2) Acts 8:37, and (3) 1 John 5:7?
4. What is the textual problem of Mark 16? Should the ending of Mark be a hindrance to our faith?

10

Restoring the New Testament Text

The New Testament text has been borne through the centuries by means of manuscripts and other materials. In the transmission of the text, mistakes were bound to appear. Our primary concern, however, is the bearing that these mistakes have on the text. The conclusion reached in the foregoing study is that practically all of the variations found among the manuscripts do not affect our present text. Although a few textual problems remain, these are explained in the footnotes of most recent translations. We are now ready to learn more about our accepted text and something of its interesting history.

Our modern Greek text may be described as a reconstructed or restored text. Only two alternatives are available if we seek to print a Greek text. Either we can select one manuscript and make it the standard text, or we can consult a number of manuscripts and authorities and by comparison reconstruct a text which we feel is like the original. If we choose the former course, we are destined to failure, for no one manuscript is free from obvious scribal errors. If we choose the latter course, we will be assured of getting much closer to the original New Testament autographs. For this reason the latter course has always been followed in the printing of the Greek New Testament. This means that our modern text is an *edition* of the New Testament text restored through all the aids of textual criticism.

Authorities for Restoring the Text

Let us suppose that we do not have a modern edition of the New Testament text. What sources shall we use in restoring the primitive text? The answer to this question will be given briefly and will partially serve as a review of preceding chapters.

1. Manuscripts. The first and primary source of information in restoring the text are manuscripts of the original language, which for the New Testament would be Greek manuscripts. But all manuscripts are not of equal weight, and therefore some may be classified as good, others as better, and a few as best. Further study of these manuscripts show that some habitually agree in their readings. They are evidently derived from a common ancestor and are called a "text type." These types of manuscripts have arisen at different times and under varying conditions. Within certain limits, their origins can be traced back to different quarters of the world, some to Alexandria in Egypt and are known as "Alexandrian"; others to Antioch of Syria, designated as "Syrian" or "Byzantine"; and still others to Western Europe, which are called "Western." Since these groups represent the wide range of textual variants, it is safe to conclude that whenever several important text types agree on a given reading, this amounts to textual certainty.

2. Versions. The Bible was translated by early Christians into many tongues. In addition to the Syriac, the Latin, and the Coptic, other versions—the Armenian, the Gothic, the Ethiopic, and the Georgian—made their appearance in the early centuries of the Christian era. Surely these translations will furnish much helpful information. They had to be made from some type of Greek text, and to find out what type of text each represents provides us with an independent line of witnesses.

3. Early Christian writers. Early Christians wrote extensively about their religion and quoted frequently from their sacred writings. They lived near the end of the first century, in the second century, and shortly afterward. Volume after volume of these "Church Fathers" have been preserved, many of which

are literally filled with quotations of the New Testament. These early Christians possessed copies of the Scriptures which naturally are older than our manuscripts today. How their many quotations read certainly tells us much concerning the ancient Bible of the primitive church. Indeed, as Professor Bruce Metzger has pointed out, "so extensive are these citations that if all other sources for our knowledge of the text of the New Testament were destroyed, they would be sufficient alone for the reconstruction of practically the entire New Testament."[1]

The manuscripts, the versions, citations from early Christian writings—these are the tools available when we undertake to restore the primitive text of the New Testament. Using these tools with discretion, it is possible to come so near the original autographs that we can all but grasp them in our hands.

The Greek New Testament in Print

To Erasmus of Rotterdam belongs the honor of editing and having published the first printed Greek New Testament. The year was 1516. The place was Basle, a Swiss city of printing and learning. The well-known printer, John Froben, had invited Erasmus to come there and oversee what was to be an epoch-making publication. Erasmus had equipped himself for the task, not only having learned Greek but having spent years in working on his own Latin translation. Through his many writings he was becoming known as Europe's most outstanding scholar.

The edition of the New Testament appeared in parallel columns, with the Greek text on the left and the Latin on the right. The Latin was not Jerome's Vulgate but an independent translation done by Erasmus. Erasmus also attached essays and numerous notes on specific passages of Scripture. Including about one thousand pages, the volume was rushed through the press and completed in about five months.

Why the hurry? Because in Spain there was already underway an edition of the Bible in Hebrew, Greek, and Latin. Undoubtedly, both Froben and Erasmus hastened to get ahead of it. As it happened, they had plenty of time, for a Spanish edition of the Bible known as the Complutensian Polyglot, done at Alcala (Complutum), was not circulated until six years later. Its New Testament portion was actually the first Greek text to be printed (1514) but not the first to be published.

In summary, several things can be said about the Erasmus New Testament. First, it was the first publication of the New Testament in Greek. Second, it was prepared on the basis of a few late Greek manuscripts that were available at the time. Third, it was edited and carried through the press in great haste. Fourth, though it would be corrected by four other editions issued by Erasmus, its many shortcomings would be perpetuated by subsequent editors of the Greek text.

Nevertheless, Erasmus was the one who led the way in valuing the Greek manuscripts over the Latin. Although frail in body, he possessed a strong spirit. In his notes on passages of Scripture, he was bold to speak out against wrongs in the Roman Church. "Bishops, seculars, monks were dragged out to judgment, and hung as on a public gibbet, in the light of the pages of the most sacred of all books. . . ."[2] For this Erasmus was much denounced, but in the eyes of others much praised. Reformation was in the air.

Following Erasmus was Robert Estienne, who Latinized his name to Stephanus. In the years 1546–51, he brought out several editions of the Greek text, the most noteworthy of which are his third and fourth editions. The latter, of 1551, is remembered especially because it was the first time that the text was divided into verses. When today we cite the New Testament by verses, we are using Stephanus' arrangement.

But it was Stephanus' third edition of 1550 that was so important. Known as "the Royal edition," in folio size (about 9 by 13 inches), it was a very beautiful edition. Its text was almost entirely that of Erasmus. From it was derived, with a few slight alterations, the text that came to be known as the "Received Text."

The work of Stephanus was forwarded by the Protestant Reformer, Theodore Beza. Although he put out a number of editions of the Greek text, in the years 1565–1604, they were essentially the text of Stephanus. Keep in mind that this was the type of text used by the translators of the King James Version.

By now the Greek text to many people had become standardized. The editions of a Dutch family of printers, the Elzevirs, confirmed this general view. Their 1633 edition assures the reader, "You have *the text* now *received by all.*"[3] Originally, this statement was printed in Latin, from which comes the expression "Textus Receptus" or "Received Text." Yet this edition was scarcely different from the Stephanus text, which was about the same as the text of Erasmus—a text based on no more than a handful of late Greek manuscripts. As more and earlier manuscripts came to light, it was inevitable for demands to be made for an improved Greek text.

Such evidence on the text began to mount. The Alexandrian Manuscript came to England in 1627. From the fifth century, it was seven hundred years earlier than the manuscripts used by Erasmus. Collations (listings of readings) of manuscripts likewise began to accumulate. Next came the gathering of evidence from the versions and then from the quotations of early Christian writers.

The Work of John Mill and Richard Bentley

This brings us to the time of John Mill and Richard Bentley. The work of Dr. John Mill of Oxford was exceptional. In the year 1707, after thirty years of Herculean labor, he issued his edition of the Greek New Testament. It was Mill's purpose to present as much of the existing evidence on the text as was possible. He gathered together previous collations, collated additional manuscripts himself, and arranged for his friends to make other collations. Along with the testimony of the manuscripts, he included abundant information from the ancient versions and Church Fathers. But Mill's edition was not a new New Testament. Mill did what his predecessors had done: he merely reprinted the Stephanus text of 1550.

Yet Mill's work provoked controversy. His collection of readings from all his sources totaled about thirty thousand variants. Daniel Whitby, among others, charged that Mill had succeeded only in making the text uncertain. Whitby thus came to the defense of the commonly accepted Received Text. Although he meant well, his unfounded arguments opened the door for those who denied the authority of Scripture. When in 1713 Anthony Collins published his *Discourse of Free-Thinking*, who was there to reply?[4]

Entering the scene was Richard Bentley, the great classics scholar and master of Trinity College, Cambridge. Bentley's response was in the form of a pamphlet entitled *Remarks upon a Late Discourse of Free-Thinking*, written under the name of *Phileleutherus*, who supposedly was a learned doctor from Leipzig. The aim of the pamphlet was twofold. On one hand Bentley sought to defend the text against those who magnified textual variations; on the other hand he wanted to speak out clearly against those, like Whitby, who defended the Received Text at all costs.

Drawing on his expert knowledge of the classics, with effective use of wit and sarcasm, and above all with an abundance of common sense, Bentley's pamphlet deserves our hearing. Given below are excerpts from a key section of *Phileleutherus*.

> Yes, but poor Dr. Mill has still more to answer for; and meets with a sorry recompense for his long labour of xxx. years. For, if we are to believe [Collins and Whitby] . . . he was *labouring* all that while *to prove the text of the Scripture precarious;* having scraped together such an immense collection of *various readings.* . . .
>
> For surely these *various readings* existed before in the several exemplars; Dr. Mill did not make and coin them, he only exhibited them to our view. If religion, therefore, was true before, though such various readings were in being, it will be as true, and consequently as safe still, though everybody sees them. Depend on't, no truth, no matter of fact fairly laid open, can ever subvert true religion. . . .
>
> In the manuscripts of the *New Testament* the variations have been noted with a religious, not to say superstitious, exact-

ness. . . . What wonder, then, if, with all this scrupulous search in every hole and corner, the varieties rise to 30,000? when in all ancient books of the same bulk, whereof the MSS. are numerous, the variations are as many or more, and yet no versions to swell the reckoning. . . . So that, if I may advise you, when you hear more of this scarecrow of 30,000, be neither astonished at the sum, nor in any pain for the text. . . . 'Tis competently exact even in the worst MS. now extant; nor is one article of faith or moral precept either perverted or lost in them; choose as awkwardly as you can, choose the worst by design, out of the whole lump of readings.[5]

Bentley himself was to go on and plan an entirely new edition of the text, but it was never completed. It would be left to the next century to fulfill this dream.

The Westcott-Hort Text

In the last few pages we have been giving some of the highlights of how the Greek text came into print, and how the Received Text became so generally accepted. We have also paused to ponder Bentley's common-sense approach to differences in the text. It is important to emphasize again the importance of the *Greek* text, for this is the source of all of our New Testament translations.

Not wanting to overlook the immense contributions of others, we must now move on to the Westcott-Hort text. Near the middle of the nineteenth century, two extraordinary things had happened, both in connection with Constantin Tischendorf. The first was his amazing discovery of the Sinaitic Manuscript; the second was his successful collation and publication of the Vatican Manuscript. That these wonderful manuscripts were now available gave added momentum both for a new edition of the Greek text and for a thorough revision of the Authorized or King James Version.

The year 1881 was an eventful year for the history of the Bible and especially for the lives of two Cambridge scholars, Brooke Foss Westcott and Fenton John Anthony Hort. On May 12 the two longtime friends and coworkers published the first of two volumes entitled *The New Testament in the Original Greek*. It was a completely new text, revised or reconstructed along the lines discussed earlier in this chapter. Lachmann, Tischendorf, and others had previously set aside the Received Text, but the work of Westcott and Hort was definitive.

On September 4 the second volume of the Greek text appeared with the subtitle *Introduction* and *Appendix*. Written by the versatile and scholarly Hort, the unassuming subtitle disguised its importance. The *Appendix*, two columns to the page in small print, consists of notes on selected textual problems. But it is the *Introduction* that is so remarkable. Brilliantly written, it comprises a monumental discussion of the principles underlying the Westcott-Hort Greek text.

It is scarcely possible to overstate the significance of this new text. Westcott and Hort gave nearly thirty years of exacting labor to this project. Their achievement was revolutionary not so much because of new ideas but rather because of the deliberate thoroughness of their work and the unquestioned principles which backed it up. No piece of evidence had been passed over unnoticed, no authority had been put aside until it was brought into proper perspective. Basically, the Westcott-Hort text represented a wholesale rejection of mass authorities and an acknowledged dependence on the Sinaitic and Vatican Manuscripts, particularly the Vatican. There have been, of course, other editions of the Greek text since Westcott-Hort; however, time has but confirmed their immense contribution to the status of our New Testament text.[6]

In the same year (1881) the English Revised Version of the New Testament appeared. The deserved attention given to this great revision brought added acclaim to the Westcott-Hort text. While the new translation was not strictly based on the Westcott-Hort edition, nevertheless Westcott and Hort had served as the best-informed textual scholars on the Revision Committee. Naturally, their influence on the committee was a dominant factor in determining the final form of the text, as is shown by the new kind of text in the revision.

(111)

I add here a personal note. Sometime ago, while working in the Manuscripts Room of the Cambridge University Library, I was going through some of Hort's personal papers. The papers include a number of Hort's handwritten notes on his preferences as to how various New Testament passages should be translated. As I was reading the papers, a little sheet fell out. Addressed to "Dr. Hort," it was signed "F. H. A. S." In a beautiful script the note read: "In a word, if we are ever to have an end of our labours, we must hold our hands now. How much, think you, should I like to see changed?"

The note recalls the frequent discussions in the Revision Committee concerning the Greek text that was to be translated. The initials F. H. A. S. unquestionably refer to F. H. A. Scrivener, who often defended readings of the Received Text. On the other hand, it was Hort who took the lead in arguing for the type of text which he and Westcott later would publish. In fact, the Westcott-Hort text, along with the English Revised Version, dealt the final blow to the Received Text upon which the King James Version is based.

Summary

Our New Testament text of today is a reconstructed or restored text. It has been reconstructed by modern scholarship from three independent lines of witnesses: the manuscripts, the versions, and the writings of early Christians (Church Fathers). In 1516 Erasmus edited and published the first New Testament in Greek, a text based on a few late manuscripts. In 1550 Robert Estienne, or Stephanus, published a beautiful edition of the Greek text that was destined to become the "Received Text." It was, however, almost identical with the text of Erasmus. For more than three hundred years, the Received Text continued to be printed and widely accepted. A great era of textual advance was marked by the publication in 1881 of a revised Greek text. This restored text was edited by Westcott and Hort and holds today, with slight modifications, a first-rate position in its field.

All new editions of the text and almost all new translations heavily depend on Westcott-Hort.

For Discussion

1. What three main sources are available to us in restoring the original text of the New Testament? Which is the most important source?
2. Briefly describe the text of Erasmus. Why is it important?
3. What is the "Received Text"? What is the origin of the expression "Textus Receptus"?
4. Who was Stephanus? What is noteworthy about the third and fourth editions of his text?
5. Identify the following: (1) John Mill, (2) Richard Bentley, and (3) *Phileleutherus*.
6. Who were the two textual scholars who produced a completely revised edition of the Greek text? When was their work published? What other famous publication came out in the same year?

11

Manuscripts from the Sand

n an earlier chapter we began our discussion of the New Testament manuscripts by going to the three important vellum uncials: the Vatican, the Sinaitic, and the Alexandrian Manuscripts. Fortunately, they are in excellent condition and are complete or almost complete copies of the New Testament. After considering other manuscripts, we referred to another group of materials that had not been discovered until recent times. We meant, of course, those manuscripts that were written on papyrus—the earliest documents of the New Testament. It is now time to direct our attention to these New Testament papyri. How and where were they discovered? What is their effect on our restored text? Do these discoveries oppose or confirm the work of Westcott and Hort?

Searching for Papyri

The modern era of the recovery of buried texts began at Herculaneum. Located on the slope of Mount Vesuvius, it was destroyed in the eruption of the volcano in A.D. 79. In the early 1700s excavations began there, and in 1750 a magnificent villa was revealed. This villa is now known as the Villa of the Papyri, for from it numerous papyrus rolls were uncovered that total (including fragments) nearly two thousand.[1]

These marvelous finds raised the possibility that other papyri might be recovered in the future. In the first part of the nineteenth century these texts began to trickle in, and by the end of the century massive numbers of papyri had appeared. The source of these documents was hot, dry Egypt, whose silting sands through the centuries had become their silent storehouse.

One area in Egypt, which has proved fruitful in exploration, is the Fayum. Located about seventy miles southwest of Cairo, it was very fertile in ancient times due to the overflow of the Nile through its canals. Following Alexander's conquests, Greek cities were built there and remained for several hundred years. Subsequently, the canals fell into disrepair, the towns were abandoned, and the desert took over.

In 1889–90, Flinders Petrie discovered in the Fayum a large number of inscribed papyri which had served as wrappings for some thirty mummies. In 1891, Frederic G. Kenyon, a young assistant in the British Museum, published a recently acquired papyrus of Aristotle's *Athenian Constitution*. In Oxford another young scholar, B. P. Grenfell, read Kenyon's publication, which turned his interest to the study of Greek papyri.

In 1895 the Egypt Exploration Fund (now Society) sent D. G. Hogarth and Grenfell to the Fayum, for trial excavations in the search of papyri. So successful were their efforts that Grenfell telegraphed A. S. Hunt, his close friend in Oxford, and asked him to join their work. Grenfell was twenty-six years old, Hunt was twenty-four. Thus began a partnership of excavation, study, and publication that was to extend for a lifetime.

The following winter of 1896–97 found Grenfell and Hunt again in Egypt, at an ancient site called Oxyrhynchus, which had been a Greek town. The Greeks named it "oxyrhynchus" after a fish by that name, which the local people considered sacred. The site was chosen by Grenfell because it was known to be a leading Christian town in the third and fourth centuries. Could there be fragments of Christian writings that would predate the oldest manuscripts of the New Testament?

After a few unimpressive weeks, Grenfell and Hunt turned to the rubbish heaps of the town that had been covered with the desert sand. Almost immediately great numbers of papyri began to appear and were gathered by the basketful.

While Grenfell frequently was overseeing the excavations, Hunt's usual task was to clean and examine the finds and prepare them for packing. After a few days, Hunt made a marvelous discovery among the fragments that had come in from the second day. He noticed an unusual Greek word, *karphos* (translated "mote" or "speck"), which reminded him of Jesus' teachings in Matthew 7:3–5. On further examination, he found on the same, small papyrus leaf other sayings attributed to Jesus, some similar to those in the Four Gospels, and others that were new.

A day or two later another remarkable discovery was made. This was a leaf from a papyrus codex, dating back to the third century. Containing the greater part of Matthew 1, it was at that time "the oldest known manuscript of any part of the New Testament."[2]

However, it was the "sayings" document that aroused great interest. Were these really the teachings of Jesus that somehow had survived the centuries? Or were they extracts from some noncanonical work? The whole question would hang in the air until another outstanding discovery of papyri was made in 1945, near Nag Hammadi, Egypt. Included in the find was the heretical (Gnostic) Gospel of Thomas with 114 "sayings," of which the Oxyrhynchus leaf later proved to be only a part.

Grenfell and Hunt continued their excavations with wonderful results. When they returned home at the end of the season, they brought back with them 280 boxes of papyri. Shortly afterward, they published their initial discovery under the title *Logia Iesu: The Sayings of Our Lord.* (*Logia* is the Greek word for "sayings.") Issued in pamphlet form, more than thirty thousand copies were sold. Grenfell and Hunt had become famous. Thereafter their work, and other searches for papyri, were permeated with an aura of fascination.

Quests for more papyri naturally followed, at Oxyrhynchus and other places. But the names of Grenfell and Hunt stand in

Courtesy of the Egypt Exploration Society, London, England

B. P. Grenfell and A. S. Hunt at Oxyrhynchus in Egypt.

the forefront, for theirs was a golden era which inaugurated the scientific search for papyri. Pioneers in papyrology, they also were superb editors. Together they issued many volumes of *The Oxyrhynchus Papyri,* and long after their deaths the volumes in this series continue to be published.

What do these volumes contain? As to the literary works, the long list of authors reads like an index of Greek literature. As to the nonliterary works, there are papyri of all sorts—tax receipts, leases, deeds, bills of sale, personal letters, and so forth.

What is there of the Greek New Testament? From Oxyrhynchus have come no less than twenty-seven manuscripts of portions of the New Testament. Twenty of these date to the second, third, or early fourth centuries. All of these, though fragmentary, are earlier than the Vatican and Sinaitic Manuscripts, and some predate them by 150 years.

The Chester Beatty Papyri

On 19 November 1931 an article appeared in *The Times* (London) with the title, "The Text of the Bible. A New Discovery."

(117)

The discovery was of a group of papyri that had been acquired by Mr. A. Chester Beatty, an American who was then living in Great Britain. The article announcing the discovery was written by Sir Frederic Kenyon.

Kenyon's name on the article gave it a stamp of authority. He had recently retired from more than forty years of work at the British Museum, having served as its director for twenty-one years. He had published many papyri and books on the Bible and textual criticism. So if Kenyon said or wrote something about the manuscripts, everyone would take notice.

The original group of Beatty papyri consists of eleven manuscripts, although at first Kenyon thought there were twelve. Eight of these contain parts of the Old Testament in Greek: considerable portions of Genesis, Numbers, and Deuteronomy, and parts of other books, including Esther, Ezekiel, and Daniel. Three manuscripts in the group are of the New Testament, which will be discussed later.

Where were these papyri discovered? Since they were bought at different times from various dealers, very little can be known with certainty. Kenyon thought that they came from the Fayum, but now it is believed that they came from the same area where the Bodmer Papyri were discovered, which will be discussed shortly.

Although some of these papyri are located elsewhere, this group is generally referred to as the Chester Beatty Papyri. In 1950 Beatty, who had made millions in copper mining, moved to Dublin, Ireland. There he built a library for his vast collections, now known as the Chester Beatty Library and Gallery of Oriental Art.

The Bodmer Papyri

The unearthing of the Beatty papyri in the 1930s was sensational. Although not nearly as well known, another amazing discovery of papyri took place in 1952—the Bodmer Papyri.

Again, the circumstances of the find remained a mystery for many years. Now it is known that these papyri were found north of the ancient city of Thebes, in Upper (Southern) Egypt. Mr. Martin Bodmer of Geneva, Switzerland, purchased the main body of the papyri, but other items went to Sir Chester Beatty and to other libraries.

The Bodmer collection is made up of a large number of papyri written in Greek and in Coptic (Egyptian). Of these, the most important are the Greek manuscripts, which encompass texts of the Old and New Testaments and other related works.

The Bodmer Papyri are of great value. The Coptic materials are very meaningful, but much more important are three manuscripts of the New Testament. They include an early text of most of the Gospel of John, an early copy of 1 and 2 Peter complete, and large portions of Luke and John from an early codex.

New Testament Papyri

Thus far we have concentrated interest on major discoveries such as the Bodmer, the Chester Beatty, and the Oxyrhynchus Papyri. Now we will consider a select number of the individual papyri. Some are mentioned only briefly, but without them an overall picture is not possible. As we proceed, remember that manuscripts are broadly classified as Alexandrian or Western or Byzantine, with a strong preference generally given to the Alexandrian form of text. In the list below, P stands for "Papyrus" and the raised numbers for the individual papyri.

P^1. This folded leaf was found by Grenfell and Hunt a few days after they began excavations at Oxyrhynchus. The text consists of more than fifteen verses of Matthew 1, mainly of the genealogy of Jesus. It is interesting that there are not many variants in this genealogical list, and that most of them are spelling differences of the proper names involved. In type, the text of P^1 is Alexandrian and is quite near to the Vatican Manuscript. Dated in the third century, it is now in Philadelphia, in the University of Pennsylvania Museum.

P[4], P[64], P[67]. Although listed as three separate fragments, we now know that they originally belonged to the same codex. The manuscript contains a good number of verses of Matthew and Luke. Recent study shows it to be more like the Vatican Manuscript than any other codex. Dating perhaps back to the late second century, it has "a very good claim to be regarded as the oldest known codex of the four Gospels."[3] At present P[75], discussed below, is its only possible rival.

P[5]. Now in the British Library, discovered by Grenfell and Hunt, dated in the third century, this manuscript was originally a codex of the Gospel of John and includes parts of various chapters. The text is Alexandrian, similar to the type of text found in the Vatican and Sinaitic Manuscripts.

P[38]. In the University of Michigan Library, part of a leaf from a codex, the text consists of portions of Acts 18 and 19. Its text, along with P[48], resembles Codex Bezae. From the close of the third century, it shows that the Bezae type of text was in Egypt at that time.

P[45]. This manuscript, along with P[46] and P[47], comprise the New Testament portion of the Chester Beatty Papyri. P[45] is a copy of the Four Gospels and Acts, but only portions of thirty leaves survive. As for its text, in the Gospels it is a mix of Alexandrian and Western types; in Acts it is nearer to the Alexandrian form of the text.

P[46]. In many ways this is a remarkable manuscript. It is the earliest text of most of the letters of Paul and is usually dated in the early third century. Of an original 104 leaves, it now has 86 leaves. Paul's letters appear in the following order: Romans, Hebrews, 1 and 2 Corinthians, Ephesians, Galatians, Philippians, Colossians, 1 and 2 Thessalonians. Portions are missing from Romans and 1 Thessalonians, and 2 Thessalonians is missing entirely.

The order of the Pauline letters is unusual and some are not present. Apparently this was a collection of Paul's letters addressed to the churches, and thus 1 and 2 Timothy, Titus, and Philemon are not included. That Hebrews is merged with the Pauline list reflects the belief then current (in Egypt?) that Paul was the author of Hebrews. Of greater importance is the

Courtesy of the University of Michigan Library, Ann Arbor, Michigan

P[46], the first leaf of the Book of Ephesians.

kind of text found in P[46]. Here, again, the codex is remarkable. Its text is often akin to the Vatican Manuscript and in general may be described as an early form of the Alexandrian text.

P[47]. This third-century codex contains about a third of the text of Revelation, with slight loss at the tops of each page. Generally speaking, its text type is Alexandrian and is especially close to that of the Sinaitic Manuscript.

P[52]. The John Rylands Library is located on a busy intersection in Manchester, England. Known for many years for its outstanding collection of books and manuscripts, its name now is frequently identified with one small piece called "the John Rylands Fragment" (P[52]). In 1920 Grenfell acquired a group of papyri for the library and began a catalog of the Rylands papyri. In 1934 C. H. Roberts of Oxford continued Grenfell's work. While sorting through the papyri, Roberts found a tiny scrap (3 1/2 by 2 1/2 inches), with a few words written on both sides, and identified it as part of John 18: 31–33, 37–38. He then carefully compared its handwriting with that of several manuscripts of known dates. On this basis he was able to date the fragment in the first half of the second century.

How we could wish that P[52] were more than a fragment! Yet it gives undeniable evidence of the circulation of the Gospel of John in Egypt, where it was found, possibly within a few years after it was written. What of the radical hypotheses that proposed a late date for John's Gospel, some as late as A.D. 170? These, as Adolf Deissmann said, "must now be recognized as hothouse plants which will quickly fade away."[4]

P[66]. The remaining papyri to be considered, including this one, constitute the leading manuscripts in the library of Martin Bodmer. Indeed, among the Biblical papyri, they are unparalleled in their length, their state of preservation, and their significance for the New Testament.

In the late 1950s many articles were printed announcing a new manuscript discovery of the Gospel of John. The manuscript was published in 1956 by Professor Victor Martin of the University of Geneva. Subsequently, supplements were issued after acquired fragments were identified. The manuscript

P[52], the first side (recto) of the John Rylands Fragment.

has almost all of the first fourteen chapters of John, with the remainder filled in partially with fragments.

This was a sensational discovery, for not only is the codex of extensive length, it is one whose age is exceptional, dating back to A.D. 200 or earlier.

What about the form of its text? Was it well copied? In some respects this is disappointing. The scribe is guilty of many careless mistakes, yet most of these were corrected by the scribe himself. Concerning its text type, though it has a mixture of different readings, it clearly fits in with the kind of text present in the Vatican Manuscript.[5]

P[72]. This Bodmer manuscript contains a miscellaneous collection of texts. It is especially important that it includes 1 and 2 Peter and Jude in complete form. Dated in the third or fourth centuries, it is the earliest known text of these letters. For the most part, its text is Alexandrian. It is closer to the Vatican Manuscript than to any other codex, especially in 2 Peter.

P[75]. Another of the Bodmer Papyri, this one is especially significant. Published in 1961, the manuscript is dated between A.D. 175 and 225. Embracing considerable portions of the Gospels of Luke and John, it is the earliest known copy of Luke and one of the earliest of John.

This early papyrus has had an extraordinary impact on textual studies. Careful examination of its text has demonstrated that P[75] is virtually the same text as that of the Vatican Manuscript (B). When Westcott and Hort issued their critical text in 1881, Hort in his introduction maintained that B preserves a "very pure line of very ancient text. . . ."[6] But later scholars took issue with Hort and maintained that B is rather a third- or fourth-century "edition" of the text. Yet if P[75] and B are practically the same, this shows conclusively that the B-type text was not an "edited" text but existed already in the second century. Thus P[75] points in the direction of Hort's view that B, except for minor points, is essentially the original text.

Conclusion

We can now look back over the recent period of papyrus discoveries and come to some definite conclusions.

1. The Greek papyri in general have had a far-reaching effect on our knowledge of the Greek *(Koine)* in which the New Testament was written. These papyri are diverse. Turning the pages of a recently published volume of papyri, one meets a variety of documents—a lease on fishing rights, a birth certificate, a

record of a slave's emancipation, and so forth. While it is possible to overemphasize the importance of these materials for the vocabulary of the New Testament, it is nevertheless true that the papyri will continue to bring a much better understanding of the meanings of certain terms and idioms in the New Testament.

2. The New Testament papyri in particular have thrown much light on the text of the New Testament. Of the nearly one hundred New Testament papyri presently known, more than fifty are of the fourth century or earlier, and more than thirty are of the third century or earlier. Further, these early papyri cover in part (some in whole) every book of the New Testament, except 1 and 2 Timothy. It should be emphasized that these papyri are the ones that just happened to survive.

3. Even the fragments of papyri are very important. We must remember that extant fragments come presumably from what were once complete manuscripts. And just a fragment of a manuscript can contribute much to our knowledge of the text.

The John Rylands Fragment may be taken as an example. Although it contains only a few words, how does it compare with today's text? Two words are spelled differently, in one case an *ei* for an *i,* in the other an *i* for an *ei*. Also it appears (here the text must be reconstructed) that in one instance a "for this" has been omitted—the difference being, "For this I have been born and I have come into the world" instead of "For this I have been born and for this I have come into the world" (John 18: 37). Except for these minor details, the oldest known portion of the text reads exactly as our modern text.

4. The recent discoveries of papyri, taken as a whole, confirm the Westcott-Hort type of text and stand opposed to the older type of text (Received Text). A good illustration of this is P[75], which is remarkably like the Sinaitic and Vatican Manuscripts, the Vatican in particular. P[66] also is similar in many ways to the kind of text found in these two great uncials. Neither of these papyri has readings characteristic of the later manuscripts. In agreement with recent translations, they do not have the verse(s) about the angel troubling the water (John 5:4) or of the adulterous woman (John 7:53–8:11). Discoveries of this

kind make us more certain than ever of the reliability of our modern text. In view of these and other findings, where the Westcott-Hort type of text has been confirmed again and again, we do not anticipate future discoveries to alter greatly the New Testament text. Other discoveries will indeed be made, but we expect them to point in the same direction.

5. The text of the New Testament, therefore, rests on solid foundations. A great part of the New Testament text has never been questioned. Westcott and Hort in the beginning of their work take extreme care in giving assurance concerning the text. They say, "The proportion of words virtually accepted on all hands as raised above doubt is very great, not less, on a rough computation, than seven-eighths of the whole. The remaining eighth therefore, formed in great part by changes of order and other comparative trivialities, constitutes the whole area of criticism." They conclude by saying that "the amount of what can in any sense be called substantial variation is but a small fraction of the whole residuary variation, and can hardly form more than a thousandth part of the entire text. Since there is reason to suspect that an exaggerated impression prevails as to the extent of possible textual corruption in the New Testament . . . we desire to make it clearly understood beforehand how much of the New Testament stands in no need of a textual critic's labours."[7]

Perhaps Westcott and Hort are speaking in hyperbolic terms. Of course, much depends on what they mean by "substantial variation." Nevertheless, the greatest of textual critics emphasize that many people *exaggerate* textual differences, and they estimate that only a thousandth part of the New Testament represents substantial variation! We might add that even where "substantial variation" may exist, not a single principle of faith or divine command is involved.

Sir Frederic Kenyon often expressed his confidence on the wholesome condition of the Biblical text. He once wrote, "The Christian can take the whole Bible in his hand and say without fear or hesitation that he holds in it the true word of God, handed down without essential loss from generation to generation throughout the centuries."[8]

Summary

In recent years the sands of Egypt have revealed numerous papyrus manuscripts, a number of which are very valuable for the New Testament. Grenfell and Hunt, two young Oxford scholars, pioneered in the scientific search for papyri. Three groups of Biblical papyri are especially important: the Oxyrhynchus Papyri, the Chester Beatty Papyri, and the Bodmer Papyri. Altogether nearly a hundred New Testament papyri are known today, more than fifty of these dating back to the fourth century or earlier. Some of these papyri are 150 years earlier than the Vatican and Sinaitic Manuscripts and thus are indispensable in filling the textual void between the great vellum uncials and the close of the apostolic age. These early papyri mainly confirm the Westcott-Hort type of text and add immeasurably to the solid foundation upon which our modern text rests.

For Discussion

1. Who were Grenfell and Hunt? What is important about their excavations at Oxyrhynchus?
2. What can you relate about the Chester Beatty and the Bodmer Papyri?
3. How many New Testament papyri are known today? How many are from the fourth century and earlier? Portions of which New Testament books are included in the papyri?
4. What is the oldest known fragment of the New Testament text? What is the significance of this fragment in terms of the text and the date of authorship?
5. How recent would a translation have to be in order to profit from the revised text of Westcott and Hort and from the Biblical discoveries mentioned in this chapter?

12

The Text of the Old Testament

n the preceding chapters we have spoken in some detail about the transmission of the Greek text of the New Testament. Again it is important to stress the importance of the Greek text, for without the words of the Greek text we are left without a foundation for our English translations. There can be no reliable English version unless there is an accurate Greek text. But we have seen that no serious objection can be laid against the Greek text, which means that our faith, based on the New Testament message, stands secure.

Our next task is to focus attention upon the text of the Old Testament. It will not be necessary to go at length in answer to the question of the Old Testament text, for the principles followed in the restoration of the New Testament text largely apply to the Old. In fact, the guidelines followed by textual critics relate to all types of literature, whether in or outside the Bible.

Text data for the Old Testament is not as vast as the multitude of witnesses on the Greek text, nor is it as comprehensive. Manuscripts of the New Testament date back to the fourth century, and a good number of the papyri reach back even farther. But this is not the case with the Old Testament. The rather recent recovery of the Dead Sea Scrolls constitutes a sensational story (told later in this chapter) with reference to the Old Testament text. Yet there remains a large gap of centuries between the time of the ancient scrolls and our earliest Hebrew manuscripts.

The Hebrew Manuscripts

Aside from the recently discovered scrolls, given below are the main manuscripts of the Hebrew Bible.

1. The Aleppo Codex. First in rank among the Hebrew manuscripts, the Aleppo Codex derives its name from the city in Syria where it had long been located. A beautifully written codex of the entire Hebrew Bible, it was finished sometime in the tenth century. Unfortunately, it is no longer complete; large sections of it were destroyed in Arab riots against the Jews.

The date was 2 December 1947, four days after the United Nations had decided to partition Palestine into a Jewish state and an Arab state. Arab mobs, looting and burning and killing, destroyed all the synagogues in Aleppo, including the 1,500-year-old Mustaribah Synagogue. Found in the ashes of this synagogue was the prized Aleppo Codex. A quarter of the manuscript had been destroyed—almost all of the Pentateuch and all of a number of other books as well. Smuggled out of Syria to Jerusalem, it is now being used as the base of a new critical edition of the Hebrew Bible to be published by Hebrew University.[1]

2. The Leningrad Codex. Of equal rank with the Aleppo Codex is the Leningrad Codex. Now the oldest complete manuscript of the Hebrew Bible, it was written in Cairo about the year 1010. It, too, is a beautiful manuscript, with pages ornately wrought.

The manuscript today is in the National Library of St. Petersburg, Russia. Although the city's name is once again St. Petersburg, the manuscript is still known as the Leningrad Codex.

The Leningrad Codex and the Aleppo Codex are both outstanding representatives of the famous Ben Asher family of scribes who lived at Tiberias in Palestine. The two manuscripts are regarded as model codices of a form of text called "the

Massoretic Text," the meaning and importance of which will be explained later. It is the Leningrad Codex that mainly underlies most editions of the modern Hebrew Bible. A splendidly photographed edition of the Leningrad Codex is now available.[2]

3. The Cairo Codex. This manuscript of the Former and Latter Prophets was written by Moses ben Asher in 895. Subsequently, it came into the possession of a Jewish sect in Jerusalem known as Karaites. After being carried off by the Crusaders and later returned, it made its way to the Karaite community in Cairo, where it remains today.

4. The Leningrad Codex of the Prophets. Written in 916, this manuscript includes Isaiah, Jeremiah, Ezekiel, and the Minor Prophets.

5. British Library Codex of the Pentateuch. Containing most of the Pentateuch, this codex is an important witness to the text. An undated manuscript, which formerly was thought to be from the ninth century, is now dated a century later.

There are, of course, many more Hebrew manuscripts. Those mentioned above are by far the most important ones. Our recent critical Hebrew texts rely upon them almost exclusively.

One may wonder why copies of the Hebrew Bible are late in comparison with the New Testament materials, especially when we recall that the Old Testament was completed several centuries before the first New Testament book was written. The answer is not difficult to find. From the Jewish standpoint, any manuscript that had been carefully copied and carefully checked with an authentic exemplar was as accurate as any other copy. In some respects the newer copy was even preferable to the older one, which would be more easily subject to wear and tear.

What happened to the older manuscripts? The Jewish scribes looked upon their copies of the Scriptures with an almost superstitious respect. This led them to give ceremonial burial to any of their texts that were damaged or defective. Their motive was to prevent the improper use of the material on which the sacred name of God had been inscribed. Before burial, however, faulty manuscripts were hidden away in a "genizah" (from Aramaic *genaz*, to hide), a kind of storeroom for manuscripts that were unusable. But however noble the intentions, the replacement of older copies with newer ones, and the burial of those discarded, have deprived us of early Hebrew manuscripts which we might otherwise have.

Early Scribal Activity

That few really old Hebrew manuscripts have survived does not indicate a lack of scribal activity. From earliest times, the Jewish scribes devoted themselves to the accurate transmission of the Biblical text. Thus there arose schools of professional scribes (cf. 1 Chron. 2:55), men who were trained in the art of writing, who were specialists in the law, and who were the supreme guardians of the text. Scribal activities involved a number of people and passed from generation to generation.

Numerous examples can be cited to show the passion of scribes for minute details of the text. When for some reason a manuscript had a letter too large or too small, these letters of unusual size were carefully duplicated. If, for example, a scribe found an extra letter in a word, he would leave the word the same but put a dot above the letter or word that he questioned. The dots show scribal uncertainty about a word or letter, but the scribes did not alter the text because the text was regarded as unalterable.

These and similar practices reflect long-standing traditions of the scribes. It was the function of *Massorah*—the Hebrew term for tradition—to guard the text. (The term is also spelled *Masorah*, the different spelling depending on varying opinions about the origin of the word.) And the scribes who transmitted the text, on the basis of their authoritative traditions, are generally known as the *Massoretes*.

The Massoretes, who go back to about A.D. 500, succeeded the earlier scribes. The Massoretes of Tiberias were the most important of the Massoretes, and the Ben Asher family of Tiberias, with whom several of the model codices are associated, are especially renowned.

(131)

The work of the Massoretes is truly significant. Their labors are spread out over a period of four or five centuries, and their contributions are many. They are perhaps best known for their system of vowels and accents which they devised for the Hebrew text. It will be remembered that all the letters in the Hebrew alphabet are consonants. Thus the Old Testament was first written without vowels. Although this may seem strange to us, it was sufficient during the many centuries Hebrew was a spoken language. When eventually Hebrew was no longer spoken, the danger was imminent that the proper pronunciation of the consonantal text might be lost. To meet the danger, the Massoretes, on the basis of their well-kept traditions, inserted vowel points above and below the lines of the text. It must be emphasized, however, that they did not bother the text itself; they only added a means by which to ensure the correct pronunciation of the text.

The Massoretes were not concerned with only such things as proper pronunciation. They also sought ways and methods by which to eliminate scribal slips of addition or omission. This they achieved through intricate procedures of counting. They numbered the verses, words, and letters of each book. They counted the number of times each letter was used in each book. They noted verses that contained all the letters of the alphabet, or a certain number of them. They calculated the middle letter, the middle word, and the middle verse of the Pentateuch; the middle verse of Psalms, the middle verse of the entire Hebrew Bible, and so forth. In fact, they counted almost everything that could be counted. With these safeguards, and others, when a scribe finished making a copy of a book, he could then check the accuracy of his work before using it.

This briefly illustrates why the work of the Massoretes is so important. The Massoretes were textual critics of the first rank. They examined and appraised carefully all the textual materials available to them and, on the basis of their abundant evidence, handed down in writing the form of the text which had been received at least several centuries before their time. Indeed, their labors were so productive and their contributions so large that our Hebrew text today is often referred to as "the Massoretic Text."

Present Status of Our Text

With the exception of recent discoveries, our earliest Hebrew manuscripts date no farther back than the ninth century, which leaves a rather wide separation of centuries between the original Old Testament autographs and our manuscripts today. This might give occasion for alarm were it not for the extreme care taken by Jewish scribes as they made copies of the Scriptures.

Long before the Massoretes, Jewish scribes were conscientiously seeking perfection in the transcription of the text. Evidence of this is found in the Talmud (Jewish civil and religious law), where rigid regulations are laid down for the preparation of copies of the Pentateuch to be used in the synagogue.

A synagogue roll must be written on the skins of clean animals, prepared for the particular use of the synagogue by a Jew. These must be fastened together with strings taken from clean animals. Every skin must contain a certain number of columns, equal throughout the entire codex. The length of each column must not extend over less than forty-eight, or more than sixty lines; and the breadth must consist of thirty letters. The whole copy must first be lined; and if three words be written in it without a line, it is worthless. The ink should be black, neither red, green, nor any other colour and be prepared according to a definite recipe. An *authentic* copy must be the exemplar, from which the transcriber ought not in the least to deviate. No word or letter, not even a *yod*, must be written from memory, the scribe not having looked at the codex before him. . . . Between every consonant the space of a hair or thread must intervene; between every word the breadth of a narrow consonant; between every new *parashah*, or section, the breadth of nine consonants; between every book, three lines. The fifth book of Moses must terminate exactly with a line; but the rest need not do so. Besides this, the copyist must sit in full Jewish dress, wash his whole body, not begin to write the name of God with a pen newly dipped in ink, and should a king address him while writing that name he must take no notice of him. . . . The rolls in which these regulations are not observed are condemned to be buried in the ground or burned; or they are banished to the schools, to be used as reading books.[3]

This strict set of regulations is a large factor that helps guarantee the accurate transmission of the Old Testament text. The Massoretes also took meticulous precautions in their vigorous effort to detect scribal errors. Variations undoubtedly existed in the manuscripts before and during the time of the Massoretes, but they could not have been major. All available evidence on the question shows that the type of text made permanent by the Massoretes was extant in the centuries that antedate the coming of Christ.[4]

The Dead Sea Scrolls

In March of 1948 the discovery of some ancient manuscripts found in the vicinity of the Dead Sea was first reported. An Arab boy, as the story goes, was looking for a lost goat and by chance stumbled on a cave. Inside the cave he found some jars containing several old leather rolls with writing on them. The boy and his companions thought the scrolls were of little value, but nevertheless took them with them. The scrolls eventually found their way to Bethlehem and were purchased in part by Metropolitan Mar Athanasius Yeshue Samuel of the Syrian Orthodox Monastery of St. Mark in Jerusalem and in part by Professor E. L. Sukenik of the Hebrew University in Jerusalem.

What were these scrolls and why are they so important? Seven rolls were in the original find. The manuscripts acquired by Mar Athanasius included (1) the Book of Isaiah, with fifty-four columns of text written on a leather scroll about twenty-four feet long, (2) a Manual of Discipline, a rule book which governed the Jewish sect (the Essenes?) responsible for producing the scrolls, (3) a commentary on the Book of Habakkuk, and (4) a work of unknown contents, which later became known as the "Genesis Apocryphon." The manuscripts obtained by Sukenik were (1) a part of the Book of Isaiah, (2) a work entitled "The War of the Sons of Light with the Sons of Darkness," and (3) a collection of Thanksgiving Hymns. All seven of these scrolls are now displayed in a museum especially built in Jerusalem for their preservation—The Shrine of the Book.[5]

Near the caves where the scrolls were found, situated on a high plateau overlooking the Dead Sea, are the ancient ruins of Qumran. Here lived the people who copied these and other scrolls and apparently later placed them in caves for safekeeping. When did this happen? Archaeological evidence shows that Qumran was inhabited from the second century B.C. to the first century A.D., a time that roughly corresponds to the dates of the scrolls.

Since the first news of discovery, numerous other scrolls have been found in ten additional caves located in the same region. In all about eight hundred scrolls, including thousands of fragments, have been uncovered. These scrolls were mostly produced by a deeply religious community of Jews who had taken up their station in the desert "to prepare the way of the Lord." Many of the scrolls concern only the peculiar beliefs of the sect, yet many others contain the text of fragmentary and even substantial portions of the Old Testament. Actually, fragments of almost every book of the Old Testament have turned up, and much material still awaits publication or evaluation or both.

Of special importance to us are scrolls of the Old Testament text. Altogether there are about two hundred, but many of these are no more than fragments. According to a recent count, the Book of Psalms is represented in the largest number of manuscripts (36), followed by Deuteronomy (29), Isaiah (21), Exodus (17), Genesis (15), and so on.[6] Of course, these numbers may need to be adjusted, depending on further publications or reassessments.

Among the many Qumran manuscripts of Biblical texts, several stand out prominently.

1QIs[a] is the usual designation for the great Isaiah Scroll, one of the manuscripts in the first discovery.[7] Dated about 100 B.C. or earlier, it is a complete copy of the Book of Isaiah, except for a few small breaks in the text. For all practical purposes, the text of this ancient scroll reads the same as the standard Massoretic Text printed in current Hebrew Bibles. There are, to be sure, a number of divergent readings represented in it, some of which are worthwhile; but the majority of readings has to do with such things as spelling, grammar, and modifications of vocabulary. Indeed, 1QIs[a] may be described as a kind of updating of the text whose older form is still retained in the Massoretic Text.

1QIs[b], also included in the first discovery, contains a number of chapters of Isaiah (41–59). It is a significant manuscript, deserving more attention than it has received. It dates back to the last half of the first century B.C. and is in remarkable agreement with the Massoretic Text. Both of these Isaiah manuscripts demonstrate that the Massoretic type of text clearly was in existence in pre-Christian times. This is the sensational part of the story. These scrolls are a thousand years earlier than the oldest of our previous Hebrew manuscripts!

Other Qumran scrolls, however, reflect readings different from the Massoretic Text. One manuscript is an early copy of Exodus, written in old Hebrew script known as "paleo-Hebrew." It is called 4QpaleoEx[m], that is, it is one of the many copies of Exodus from Cave 4. This Exodus copy is from the early part of the second century B.C. and contains some forty columns from an original fifty-seven. At times this manuscript shows agreements with early forms of the Samaritan Pentateuch and the Septuagint (discussed in the next chapter).

Two manuscripts of the Book of Samuel are especially interesting. One (4QSam[a]) from the first century B.C. has preserved in fragmentary form portions (about 10 percent) of 1 and 2 Samuel. The other (4QSam[b]) has parts of several chapters of 1 Samuel and dates perhaps as early as the third century B.C. These manuscripts have attracted considerable attention because, in agreement with the Septuagint, at times

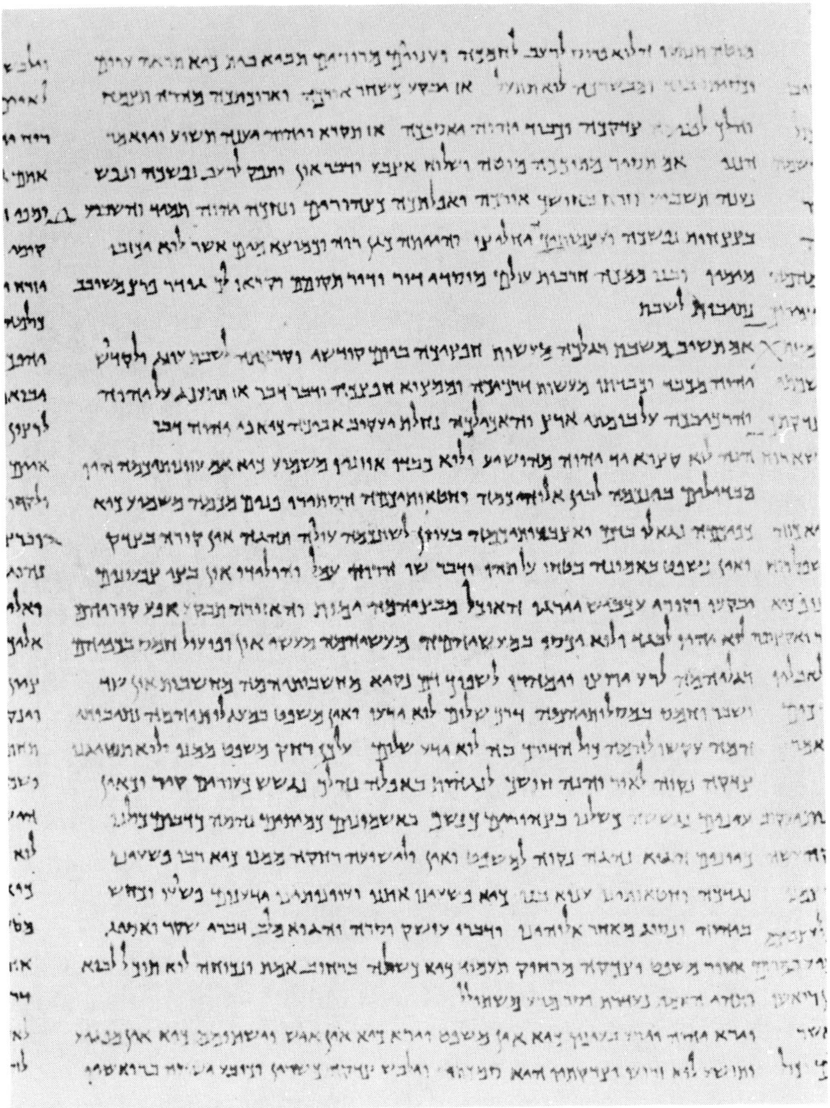

IQIs[a], a column of the Isaiah Scroll.

they appear to offer better readings than those of the Massoretic Text. But such matters continue to be studied.

Conclusion

With a mass of information on the text of the Old Testament,
what are we to think? Is it possible to sort through all of this
and come to some definite conclusions?

Even though the picture is not complete, since some materials
remain unpublished, a number of things are clear and can be
stated with confidence.

1. The differences among the scrolls, with a few having
agreements with the Samaritan Pentateuch and/or the Septuagint, should not be surprising. Bible students know that
quotations in the New Testament from the Septuagint are
not exactly like those in the Hebrew-based Old Testament.
Most of the differences are simply translation differences,
but others point to a different type of text being used. At
Qumran various types of texts are represented, which may
mean (1) that at that time and at certain points the text was
somewhat free, or (2) that the text then existed in several
distinct text types, or (3) that some of the texts were of the
more "popular" type that were never accepted by normative Judaism. Regardless, the positive outcome is that some
readings from these ancient scrolls can be used to clarify or
supplement occasional obscurities in the Massoretic Text.
Whenever this occurs, recent translations inform the reader
in appropriate footnotes.

2. The differences among the manuscripts may be viewed
from separate angles. One may describe a manuscript as
though it varies greatly from the standard text; another may
speak of the same manuscript as if it is like the standard text.
The difference is only a matter of perspective. Textual critics
must necessarily be concerned with the precise form of a given
word—how it is spelled or if it has any other minor differences.
But as we have seen earlier, these things do not affect the overall
message of the text.

3. The vast majority of the manuscripts found near the Dead Sea are closely akin to or are virtually identical with the Massoretic Text. Among the scrolls, for example, there are some twenty manuscripts of Isaiah. Every one of these is basically a Massoretic type of text. This is also true of other manuscripts that have been found elsewhere in the Judean desert—every one is a virtual copy of the Massoretic Text.

The remarkable agreement of the texts of the scrolls and our text today is well illustrated by the sixth chapter of Isaiah. Comparing the great Isaiah Manuscript (1QIs[a]) with our present Hebrew text, we are able to count thirty-seven variant readings in this chapter. But practically all of these variants are no more than spelling differences. Only three of them are large enough to be reflected in an English translation, and of these not one is significant. These three variants are: "they were calling" instead of "one called to another" (v. 3); "holy, holy," instead of "holy, holy, holy," (v. 3); and "sins" for "sin" (v. 7). In these cases our present text (Massoretic Text) is unquestionably better than that found in the Isaiah Manuscript.

We may add the statements of two outstanding scholars on the Old Testament text.

Bleddyn J. Roberts says:

> ... the authenticity of the Massoretic text stands higher than at any time in the history of modern textual criticism, a standpoint which is based on a better assessment of the history of the Jewish transmission.[8]

J. Weingreen writes:

> It should therefore be stated explicitly that, when we survey the Hebrew Bible as a whole, the incidence of copyists' errors is statistically very few indeed. Even allowing for the intrusion of occasional errors in the received Hebrew text, it is remarkable how faithfully it was transmitted.[9]

(139)

Summary

The Aleppo Codex and the Leningrad Codex are regarded as our very best Hebrew manuscripts, but they date no farther back than to the tenth and eleventh centuries. This might prove to be a difficult barrier for the Old Testament text were it not for the safeguards devised and followed by the Massoretes and the strict rules observed by earlier Jewish scribes. The Massoretes were so important in the transmission of the text that our modern Hebrew Bible is generally known as "the Massoretic Text." The Biblical documents of the Dead Sea Scrolls are nothing short of sensational. The two Isaiah scrolls and many others as well, even though they go as far back as the B.C. era, demonstrate that the Old Testament text was well preserved and accurately handed down to us.

For Discussion

1. What accounts for the difference of age between the earliest Old Testament manuscripts and the earliest New Testament manuscripts?
2. Who were the Massoretes? What did they do to secure the proper pronunciation of the Hebrew text?
3. List some of the devices used by the Massoretes to safeguard the accurate transmission of the text.
4. What are some of the regulations which governed the preparation of copies of the Pentateuch for synagogue use?
5. What are some of the most important documents of the Dead Sea Scrolls? How does their age compare with the age of previous Hebrew manuscripts?
6. Discuss the accuracy of our Hebrew text today in relation to the Dead Sea Scrolls. Are there any problems here? How do the scrolls confirm the reliability of our accepted Old Testament text?

Ancient Versions:
The Old Testament

he most important materials in the establishing of a text are those that are found in the original language of the text. For the Old Testament text, then, the basic sources will always be the Hebrew manuscripts. Nevertheless, additional materials often can cast much light on the text. Here we refer to the ancient versions or translations of the Old Testament. As independent witnesses to the text, they are helpful in several ways. First, the versions tell us something of the kind of text in use prior to the time of the Massoretes, for some of them go as far back as several centuries B.C. Second, the versions, when used with discretion, can clarify or complement the Massoretic Text when it appears to be defective. Third, the versions very often are parallel with the Massoretic Text and give it increased credibility.

We proceed now to learn more about the ancient versions. The most important of these are the Septuagint, the Aramaic Targums, the Syriac, and the Latin. Some of these will be treated rather briefly, including the Samaritan Pentateuch, which strictly speaking is not a version at all. Pride of place belongs to the Septuagint, which will be dealt with in more detail.

Samaritan Pentateuch

The Samaritan Pentateuch is not a translation but is a form of the Hebrew text itself. Its beginning can be traced back to about 400 B.C., when the Samaritans separated themselves from the Jews and built their sanctuary on Mount Gerizim, near Shechem. As a result the Samaritans adopted their own form of the Hebrew Scriptures and counted as authoritative only the five books of Moses.

In one sense the Samaritan Pentateuch presents a problem, for it bears some six thousand variants from the Massoretic Text. But on examination the problem is not as great as it might appear. Most of the variants have to do with spelling and grammatical differences and similar small details. Many other differences are due to the peculiar beliefs of the Samaritan community. For example, after the Ten Commandments in Exodus 20 and Deuteronomy 5, the Samaritan Pentateuch inserts a long passage, commanding that the Israelites build an altar on Mount Gerizim. In Deuteronomy 27:4, instead of Mount Ebal the Samaritan Pentateuch reads Mount Gerizim. With such views it is not surprising that the Samaritans rejected the rest of the Old Testament, which often praises Jerusalem and Zion.

Yet overall there are few major differences between the Hebrew and Samaritan Pentateuchs, which means that to a high degree the Samaritan Pentateuch confirms the traditional Hebrew text. Of course, in those cases where the Samaritan Pentateuch differs, and where these cases are supported by the Septuagint, textual critics must and do take notice.

Aramaic Targums

Nehemiah 8 tells of the gathering of the people to hear the reading of the law of Moses. According to verses 5–7, Ezra read from the law, and the Levites explained it to the people. Verse 8 says, "So they read from the book, from the law of God, with interpretation. They gave the sense, so that the people understood the reading" (NRSV). This appears to be the earliest reference to an oral paraphrase of Scripture called *targum.*

After the period of the Jewish exile in Babylon, Aramaic became the spoken language of the Jews. In order for the people to understand the reading of Scripture in public worship, it was necessary for it be translated or paraphrased in Aramaic. The word that refers to a translation is *targum.*

In the synagogues the Targums were always oral, while the honored Hebrew text was always read from a scroll. This was a strict rule, lest the paraphrase be confused with the authoritative text. Accordingly, over the centuries a number of Targums arose, and later they were committed to writing, at least by the beginning of the Christian era. By the fifth century two official Targums had emerged, *Targum Onkelos* of the Pentateuch and *Targum Jonathan* of the Prophets. Of the two, Targum Onkelos is considered the greater authority. Both are quite literal in their efforts of translation.

One noticeable feature of the Targums is their preference for paraphrase in Biblical references to God. In Genesis 3:8, instead of "the sound of the Lord God walking in the garden," Targum Onkelos has "the sound of the word of the Lord God walking in the garden." Mount Sinai, called "the mountain of God," is paraphrased as "the mountain upon which the glory was revealed" (Exod. 3:1). Similarly, when Isaiah says "I saw the Lord," the paraphrase reads, "I saw the glory of the Lord" (Isa. 6:1).

Several fragments of Targums have been found at Qumran, which consistently bear witness to the Massoretic type of text.

Syriac Peshitta

While the Aramaic Targums were written in a dialect called Western Aramaic—the language spoken by the Jews during the time of Christ—other translations were made in the dialect of Eastern Aramaic called Syriac. Although there were several Syriac versions of the New Testament, mainly one has survived in the Old Testament, the *Peshitta,* that is, the *simple* version.

The Syriac Old Testament was begun very early, probably as early as the middle of the first century A.D. Who the translators were, whether Jewish or Christian, is not known. Perhaps both had their share. In its earliest form the Peshitta is in close agreement with the Massoretic Text. Later, there is considerable evidence where it has been unduly influenced by readings of the Septuagint. Nevertheless, the Peshitta is an important tool for the textual criticism of the Old Testament.

Latin Vulgate

Ordinarily, this is the place where the Septuagint would be discussed, but we will set it aside for now and return to it later. In the meantime, let us complete the story of Jerome's work on the Latin Vulgate (see chapter 6).

With reference to the Latin versions, we have seen that there are two main types, the Old Latin and the Vulgate. The Old Latin dates back to about A.D. 150, but it has definite limitations because it is based on the Septuagint. The Latin Vulgate, on the other hand, is more valuable because it goes back to the original Hebrew. This is where we pick up the story of Jerome.

Jerome had been commissioned to revise the Old Latin, and by the year 384 he had completed the Gospels and perhaps, a little later, other portions of the New Testament. For the next few years in Bethlehem, where he had moved, he continued his work by translating several books of the Old Testament. These, however, were rendered from the Septuagint and not from the Hebrew. But the more Jerome learned Hebrew the more he was convinced that the ultimate authority for any Old Testament book could be nothing but the Hebrew. It was a major step, therefore, when he began a fresh translation of the Old Testament directly from the Hebrew. And this is exactly what we have in the Latin Vulgate Old Testament.

Jerome spent about fifteen years (390–405) in putting the Old Testament into Latin. First he translated Samuel and Kings. Next appeared the Psalms, which previously he had revised twice. Then came the Prophets and Job, followed by Ezra and Chronicles, and finally the remaining books of the Old Testament.

How would Jerome's work be regarded? Earlier we saw that he was reproached for his revision of the Gospels. His revision of the Old Testament brought him more distress. Generations of Christians had been reading their Latin translations based on the Septuagint. How could Jerome be so presumptuous as to alter their translations?

Several of Jerome's prefaces to the Old Testament books mention his critics. In his preface to Job he assures his "barking critics" that he does not intend to belittle the Septuagint but only to bring out from the Hebrew what is otherwise obscure. The preface to Samuel and Kings he calls a "helmeted preface," because in it he arms himself against his opponents.

In this preface Jerome explains his views on the Apocrypha (see chapter 15). He declares that as there are twenty-two letters in the Hebrew alphabet, so there are twenty-two books of the Hebrew canon. He then lists the twenty-two books which, though counted differently, are the same as our thirty-nine.

Although Jerome hurriedly translated Tobit and Judith for his friends, he excluded them from the canon because they did not meet the benchmark of what he called "the Hebrew truth." Nevertheless, contrary to Jerome, the books of the Apocrypha, handed down in their Old Latin form, were retained in the Latin Bible.

Summing up, we can say that Jerome was qualified as a scholar in a way that other Christian scholars were not. Because of his knowledge of Hebrew, he was able to translate the Old Testament from the original language. Although he worked before the time of the Massoretes, the Hebrew manuscripts he used are almost identical with the Massoretic Text.

The Septuagint

We will now have to step back in time in order to consider one of the most important Bible translations ever made—the translation of the Hebrew Old Testament into Greek. Known in manuscripts as "according to the seventy," we generally refer to it by its Latin name, "Septuagint."

The Letter of Aristeas supposedly tells us about the origin of the Septuagint.[1] The letter is tedious and lengthy, now arranged in more than three hundred verses. Aristeas, who apparently is an Alexandrian Jew, writes to his brother Philocrates and tells him of what took place at the court of Ptolemy II (285–247 B.C.). According to the letter, the king asks Demetrius, his librarian, to arrange to have the Jewish Law translated and added to the royal collection of books. So a letter is sent to Eleazar, the Jewish high priest, asking for help to translate the Law. Aristeas himself is one of the two men chosen to carry the request to Jerusalem.

Aristeas describes all of this, even details about the Jewish temple, the priests, the countryside, and so on. Seventy-two elders, six from each of the twelve tribes, are selected as translators and dispatched to Egypt, carrying with them a beautiful copy of the Law. Aristeas lists the names of the translators. For some reason the original number of seventy-two has been rounded down to seventy—the Septuagint.

On arriving in Alexandria, the king furnishes them with a banquet of seven days, where each translator's wisdom is proved by questions from the king. After this the king provides them with wonderful accommodations near the sea, probably on the island of Pharos. On Pharos stood the famous recently constructed lighthouse—one of the seven wonders of the ancient world. Under the shadow of the lighthouse the translators complete their work in seventy-two days, which, when read to the assembled Jews at Alexandria, is approved as accurate.

What are we to think of the Letter of Aristeas? Is it fact or fiction?

In response we should say that the whole question of Aristeas is complex. Unquestionably, there are historical problems here. For example, we are not sure whether Demetrius was the librarian of Ptolemy II or Ptolemy I. Moreover, the letter has an affected tone that often reads more like legend than fact. On the other hand, it has long been recognized that Aristeas preserves at least a substratum of truth on how the Septuagint began.

What, then, can we learn from this letter? The following seems either factual or plausible concerning the Septuagint.

Aristeas describes the origin of the Septuagint with the translation of the Pentateuch. This was done in Alexandria, where there was a large Jewish population and where a translation from Hebrew to Greek would be needed. Ptolemy II in some way may have been connected with the translation; he was well known as a patron of literature. Demetrius likewise may have been involved. He may have suggested the translation to Ptolemy I, but the project may not have been completed until the beginning of the reign of Ptolemy II.[2]

There are other factors to consider. According to Aristeas, the Pentateuch was translated in the third century B.C. This date is quite reasonable. The names of the translators fit in with known names in the third century B.C.; and Philo reports that in his day, the first century A.D., an annual festival was still being held on Pharos to honor the place "in which the light of that version first shone out."[3]

Since Aristeas refers only to the translation of the Jewish Law, we have no information on how or when the remainder of the Old Testament was translated. We can only infer that as the need arose certain individuals or groups translated the various books, probably the Prophets (Former and Latter) first and the Writings later. How long this took no one knows. But we are practically certain that before the dawn of the Christian era, and perhaps well before, the entire Old Testament was accessible in Greek.

Questions are often raised about the Septuagint. As a translation, is it good or bad or something in between? The answer is not easy to give, for the Septuagint itself presents many problems. For one thing, we are not sure that we can speak of an *original* Septuagint text. Was there one early Greek version or several? Or were there various "editions" of the Septuagint? Further, how does the Septuagint relate to the Hebrew text? And, knowing that the Septuagint did not come about all at once, how is it possible to characterize it?

(147)

Addressing the last question first, generally speaking it can be said that the Septuagint represents a mean between the extreme of wooden literalness and random paraphrase. Unquestionably, the Semitic or Hebrew element shines through in many sections. On the other hand, its Greek is often a good expression of the common *(Koine)* Greek of that period. In particular, the Pentateuch has been carefully done, its vocabulary being largely typical of what was current in Egypt in the third and second centuries B.C.[4]

Concerning the question of how the Septuagint compares with the Hebrew text, again the answer cannot be stated simply. Since Greek was so widely spoken during this time, it would be natural to expect that a number of Greek translations were made and were circulated in the Mediterranean world. The fact is that the Septuagint never seems to have been a unified and carefully guarded form of the Old Testament text. These matters should be understood before discussing any problem of Septuagint versus Hebrew.

At various places the textual differences between the Greek and Hebrew texts are considerable. Exodus 35–40 reveals substantial rearrangements in the Septuagint text. Judges preserves two forms of the Greek text. Samuel-Kings presents here and there different forms of the Greek and Hebrew texts. In Jeremiah the Greek text is one-eighth shorter than that of the Hebrew and places the oracles against the nations (chaps. 46–51) after 25:13. Of course, other passages could be cited.

What can be said about such differences? Let us take two of the more difficult problems. The cases of 1 and 2 Samuel and Jeremiah are as challenging as any, and here we cannot expect easy answers. But a few things must be kept in mind.

Among the recently discovered scrolls, at least four (sometimes counted as parts of six) contain portions of Jeremiah. Dating from the third to the first century B.C., they preserve altogether forty-nine sections of text from thirty chapters. The vast majority of these agree with or are closely akin to our modern Hebrew text (the Massoretic Text). Only three of the forty-nine sections resemble the Septuagint. Incidentally, the only manuscript that includes a section of the nations' oracles places it at the end of the book, in agreement with the Hebrew arrangement as opposed to that of the Septuagint.

Still, the possibility must be granted that there were different forms of the Hebrew text of Jeremiah. The same may be said for the text of 1 and 2 Samuel. The Dead Sea Scrolls include four fragmentary manuscripts of Samuel, of which two in particular are more closely related to the Septuagint than to the Hebrew. How or on what basis to explain these differences remains a moot point among textual critics. In such cases, where there are important differences, the reader will find the relevant text data in the footnotes of recent translations.

One or two other things need emphasis. Although there are numerous textual variations between the Septuagint and the Hebrew text, the great majority of these are minor. Often it is not mentioned how very much the Septuagint supports the Hebrew text. Yet even when the Septuagint differs and offers a better reading, nonetheless it never replaces the Hebrew as the standard form of the text. Because it is a translation, the Septuagint always remains secondary. Only with great care, then, can one speak of "the authority of the Septuagint."

Apart from its bearing on the text, there are a number of reasons why we have taken time to explore the Septuagint. Its influence has been very great.

Genesis, Exodus, Leviticus, Numbers, and Deuteronomy are names that have come into our Bible from the Septuagint by way of the Latin Vulgate. Likewise, the grouping of books into Law, History, Poetry, and Prophets as well as the subdividing of books into 1 and 2 Samuel, 1 and 2 Kings, and so forth, are due to the Septuagint.

Beyond this, the Septuagint will always hold interest among Christians. For a while it was the only Bible for the early church. It was the text most often quoted by the apostles and inspired writers of the New Testament. Paul, for example, did not write peasant Greek or soldier Greek but wrote as a man with the Septuagint in his blood.[5]

Students of the New Testament, therefore, must always draw on the background of the Old Testament. Many New Testament terms and phrases come right out of the Septuagint, including words like "apostle," "atonement," "covenant," "faith," "forgiveness," "glory," "law," "peace," "redemption," "righteousness," and "truth."

Today we can only be grateful for the Septuagint. The New Testament was written in Greek, but before it came the Old Testament translated into Greek. It was in God's providence that the Septuagint by its language and vocabulary would open up the way for the gospel in a world dominated by Greek.

Summary

The ancient versions of the Old Testament, because they are translations, must always be considered secondary witnesses to the text. Yet they offer an independent line of testimony and at times can add welcomed light to the Hebrew text. The most important of these versions are the Septuagint, the Aramaic Targums, the Syriac, and the Latin Vulgate. Besides these is the Samaritan Pentateuch, which is an early form of the Hebrew text for the five books of Moses. The Septuagint continues to receive much scholarly attention. The Letter of Aristeas has preserved basic information on its origin, but there are difficulties with the letter. And sometimes there are difficulties when the Septuagint is compared with the Hebrew text, but such textual differences can usually be solved with care and good judgment. The Septuagint remains of special interest to Christians because (1) it was the Bible of the early church, (2) its background is fundamental for understanding the New Testament, and (3) its language prepared the way for evangelism in the Greek world.

For Discussion

1. Of what value are the ancient versions for the text of the Old Testament? In what ways are they limited?
2. What is the Samaritan Pentateuch? What are its merits and its shortcomings?

3. What are the Aramaic Targums? Why were they necessary? What is a targum?
4. What is especially significant about Jerome's role as a translator of the Old Testament?
5. Why is it important to study about the Septuagint? How is the expression "the authority of the Septuagint" to be understood and applied?

The Canon of the Scriptures

 uch of the preceding study has been given to the transmission of the Bible text—how and under what conditions the text has come down to us, and how we can be sure that we have the exact words of this text. It is now time to take up another phase of the history of the Bible: the collection of books that comprise *Scripture*. Many religious books were written during the period of the Old and New Testaments. Which of these books rightfully belongs to the Bible, and which should be excluded from it? On what grounds are some writings to be accepted as Scripture and others to be rejected? The answer to these questions can be found in the study of what is known as the "canon" of the Scriptures.

The English word "canon" goes back to the Greek word *kanon* and then to the Hebrew *qaneh*. Its basic meaning is "reed," our English word "cane" being derived from it. Since a reed was sometimes used as a measuring rod, the word *kanon* came to mean a standard or rule. It was also used to refer to a list or index and when so applied to the Bible denotes the list of books which are received as Holy Scripture. Thus if one speaks of the "canonical" writings, one is speaking of those books which are regarded as having divine authority and which comprise our Bible.

There is a difference between the canonicity of a book and the authority of that book. A book's canonicity depends on its authority. When Paul, for example, writes to the Corinthians, his letter is to be acknowledged as possessing divine authority (1 Cor. 14:37). This letter had authority from the moment he wrote it, yet it could not be referred to as canonical until it was received in a list of accepted writings formed sometime later. At a later time it was accepted as canonical because of its inherent authority. A book first has divine authority based on its inspiration, and then attains canonicity due to its general acceptance as a divine product. No church council by its decrees can make the books of the Bible authoritative. The books of the Bible possess their own authority and, indeed, had this authority long before there were any councils of the church.

The Canon of the Old Testament

Good evidence exists in the New Testament which shows that by the time of Jesus the canon of the Old Covenant had been fixed. It cannot be questioned that Jesus and his apostles time after time quote from a distinctive body of authoritative writings. They designate them as "the Scripture" (John 7:38; Acts 8:32; Rom. 4:3), "the Scriptures" (Matt. 21:42; John 5: 39; Acts 17:11), "the Holy Scriptures" (Rom. 1:2), "the Sacred Writings" (2 Tim. 3:15), and so forth. They often introduce their quotations with "it is written," that is, it stands firmly written and it is indisputably true. Such references are not studiously registered but simply reflect their customary manner of speaking. If some writings were "Scripture," others were not. If some writings were canonical, others were noncanonical.

Jesus himself gives us some clear indications about the extent of the Old Testament canon. When applying the Scriptures and their fulfillment to himself, he speaks of "the law of Moses and the prophets and the psalms" (Luke 24:44). This threefold division is undoubtedly equivalent to the three divisions of the Hebrew Scriptures: the Law, the Prophets, and the Writings (see chapter 2).

On another occasion Jesus not only alludes to this threefold arrangement but points to the books contained in this arrangement. He once spoke of the time "from the blood of Abel to the blood of Zechariah who perished between the altar and the sanctuary" (Luke 11:51; cf. Matt. 23:35), thus referring to the martyrs of the Old Testament. The first martyr of the Old Testament, of course, was Abel and the last martyr was Zechariah (2 Chron. 24:20–21). We should keep in mind that the Jewish order of the Old Testament differs from ours, and that Chronicles is placed at the end of the Hebrew Bible. Thus the Old Testament Jesus knew was a collection of writings reaching from Genesis to Chronicles, with all the other books in between, a collection which embraces the same books as in our Old Testament today.[1]

Some scholars have argued that toward the close of the first century Jewish leaders at Jamnia (located near the coast of Palestine) determined the limits of the Old Testament canon. However, all we can be sure of is that discussions were held in Jamnia about certain books such as Ecclesiastes and the Song of Solomon. The canon was substantially fixed long before Jamnia, and discussions there did not admit certain books into the canon but allowed these books to remain.[2]

Additional evidence on the Old Testament canon comes from Josephus, a well-known Jewish historian of the first century. In his *Against Apion,* written about A.D. 95, he defends the Jews by arguing that they possessed an antiquity unmatched by the Greeks:

> . . . it follows that we do not possess myriads of inconsistent books, conflicting with each other. Our books, those which are justly accredited, are but twenty-two, and contain the record of all time. Of these, five are the books of Moses, comprising the laws and traditional history from the birth of man down to the death of the lawgiver. This period falls only a little short of three thousand years. From the death of Moses until Artaxerxes, who succeeded Xerxes as king of Persia, the prophets subsequent to Moses wrote the history of the events of their own times in thirteen books. The remaining four books contain hymns to God

and precepts for the conduct of human life. From Artaxerxes to our own time the complete history has been written, but has not been deemed worthy of equal credit with the earlier records, because of the failure of the exact succession of the prophets.

Josephus goes on to state how highly the Jews esteemed their Scriptures:

> We have given practical proof of our reverence for our own Scriptures. For, although such long ages have now passed, no one has ventured either to add, or to remove, or to alter a syllable; and it is an instinct with every Jew, from the day of his birth, to regard them as the decrees of God, to abide by them, and, if need be, cheerfully to die for them.[3]

We can draw several conclusions from Josephus.

1. The number of books looked upon as having divine authority is carefully limited to twenty-two. By joining Ruth to Judges and Lamentations to Jeremiah, and remembering that the Jews enumerated their books differently, the twenty-two books mentioned by Josephus are the same as the thirty-nine books in our Bible today.

2. The division of the books is according to a three-part pattern. Although individual books are included in different categories, they form a threefold grouping similar to the Law, the Prophets, and the Writings.

3. The time covered in these books is expressly limited. Josephus believed that the canon extended from Moses to Artaxerxes (464–424 B.C.). This corresponds with the Jewish belief that prophetic inspiration ceased with Malachi, who apparently was a contemporary of Ezra and Nehemiah.[4] This was the period of Artaxerxes. Others indeed wrote later, but their writings are not on a par with the earlier writings. In other words, according to Josephus, the canon is closed.

4. The text of these books is sacred. No one has dared to cancel or alter it, since to every Jew these writings are "decrees of God."

Confirmation of the number of books accepted by Josephus comes from early Christian writers such as Origen and Jerome. In the third century A.D., Origen counts twenty-two books of the Old Testament. Giving both their Hebrew and Greek titles, he lists them as follows: (1–5) the Five Books of Moses, (6) Joshua, (7) Judges-Ruth, (8) 1 and 2 Samuel, (9) 1 and 2 Kings, (10) Chronicles, (11) Ezra-Nehemiah, (12) Psalms, (13) Proverbs, (14) Ecclesiastes, (15) Song of Solomon, (16) Isaiah, (17) Jeremiah-Lamentations, (18) Daniel, (19) Ezekiel, (20) Job, and (21) Esther.[5] Origen omits from his list the Book of the Twelve (the Minor Prophets), but this is clearly an accidental omission since it is necessary to make up his own number of twenty-two.

At the end of the fourth century, Jerome staunchly maintains that the number of books in the Hebrew Old Testament must be no more than twenty-two. He cannot admit other books because they are not in the Hebrew canon.

The Canon of the New Testament

About the middle of the second century, a Christian writer, Justin Martyr, stated that on Sundays in the Christian worship assemblies the "memoirs of the apostles" were read together with the "writings of the prophets."[6] It is evident, then, that not long after the close of the apostolic age the New Testament writings were being read generally among the churches. What brought this about? How was it possible that within a short time the writings of the apostles were being used for public reading as well as the writings of the Old Testament prophets?

When the church of Christ was first established, it had no thought of a New Testament. Its Bible was the Old Testament and its new teachings were based on the authority of Christ as personally mediated through the apostles. Soon, inspired men began to put in writing divine regulations both for churches and for individuals. It was inevitable that these written instructions would become normative, for Christians could not have less respect for them than for their Christ. Thus Paul's letters were carefully gathered into a single whole; next came the collection of the Four Gospels, and then all the others followed.

Because these collections were made at different times and places, the contents of the various collections were not always the same. This helps to explain why not all of the New Testament books were at first received without hesitation; while in other instances uncertainty of a book's authorship, as in the case of Hebrews, presented temporary obstacles to universal acceptance. This was the exception, however, rather than the rule, and gradually each book on its own merit—not without, Christians believe, a guiding Providence—took its place in the accepted canon of New Testament Scripture.

If it is no later than the middle of the second century when the apostles' letters became widely read in public meetings, it is no later than the last half of that century when substantial lists of the New Testament books appear. One of these early lists is known as the Muratorian Fragment. Since its date has been unsuccessfully challenged,[7] it remains an important second-century witness to the canon. The Fragment derives its name from L. A. Muratori, who first discovered the list and published it in the eighteenth century. Part of this early list of New Testament books has been lost. The Gospel of Luke is first mentioned by name, but it is referred to as the "third" Gospel, indicating that Matthew and Mark were at the head of the list. Then follow John, Acts, thirteen letters of Paul, Jude, two letters of John,[8] and Revelation. The only books not included in the list are Hebrews, James, 1 and 2 Peter, and perhaps 3 John.[9] Notwithstanding these omissions this early list provides in broad outline the substance of our modern New Testament.

It should be stated, however, that the Muratorian Fragment accepts two other books, the Wisdom of Solomon and the Apocalypse of Peter. The Fragment qualifies the latter by saying that "some of our people" do not want to have it read in the church. But other books were excluded. Among these are the Shepherd of Hermas, which was not accepted because it was written, as the Fragment says, "quite lately in our time in the city of Rome" (c. A.D. 140). It was to be read in church but not "among the prophets, whose number is settled, or among the apostles till the end of time." Still other books, the Fragment notes, are heretical and are to be entirely repudiated.

In the third century Origen adds his witness on the New Testament books. Although he wrote numerous sermons and commentaries on practically everything Biblical, most of these have not survived. Eusebius, who wrote his *Ecclesiastical History* about the year 340, gathered together a number of Origen's statements concerning the canon.[10] But since these are not complete, one has to go here and there among Origen's extant writings to get his views.

Origen knows only four Gospels and lists them in the order of Matthew, Mark, Luke, and John, with his comments on each: "The Church possesses four Gospels, heresy a great many. . . ."[11] Likewise, he undoubtedly accepts Acts, the thirteen letters of Paul, 1 Peter, 1 John, Jude, and Revelation. About the other books, Hebrews, James, 2 Peter, 2 and 3 John, Origen is hesitant. He quotes from Hebrews numbers of times, but concedes that some churches do not accept it. Second Peter, he says, is "possibly" from Peter, "but this is disputed." Concerning 2 and 3 John, John "has possibly also left a second and third epistle, but not all consider these to be genuine." Yet with these reservations it is remarkable how similar Origen's list is with that of the Muratorian Canon.

But Origen lists the canon differently elsewhere. In his *Homilies on Joshua,* preserved only in a later Latin translation, after describing the fall of the walls of Jericho, he compares the New Testament authors with the trumpets of Christ.

> So too our Lord Jesus Christ . . . sent his apostles as priests carrying well-wrought trumpets. First Matthew sounded the priestly trumpet in his Gospel. Mark also, and Luke, and John. . . . Peter moreover sounds with the two trumpets of his Epistles; James also and Jude . . . and John gives forth the trumpet sound through his Epistles and Revelation; and Luke while describing the deeds of the apostles. Latest of all . . . [Paul] thundering on the fourteen trumpets of his Epistles, threw down, even to the very foundations, the walls of Jericho.[12]

(158)

Thus with great oratorical flourish Origen lists the same twenty-seven books that we have in our New Testament today. We may wonder why Origen varies in his lists of the canon, but since he wrote so prolifically, it is not surprising that over many years he expressed different views. Regardless, it is important to keep in mind that his New Testament of the third century is very much like ours today.

In the fourth century all these matters are pretty well brought to a conclusion. The testimony on the canon by Eusebius, the great church historian, is important, but it does not bring us much farther along the line. Eusebius distinguishes three categories of books: (1) those that are universally acknowledged, (2) those that are disputed, and (3) those that are rejected. The books acknowledged by all are the Four Gospels, Acts, fourteen letters of Paul, 1 John, 1 Peter, and Revelation.[13] The disputed books include James, Jude, 2 Peter, and 2 and 3 John, but these are "recognized by the majority." The rejected books, among others, are the Shepherd of Hermas, the Epistle of Barnabas, and the Teachings of the Apostles.

In A.D. 367 Athanasius of Alexandria published a list of twenty-seven books of the New Testament that were accepted in his time, and these are the same twenty-seven that are recognized today. Immediately after his list of books, Athanasius adds: "These are the springs of salvation. . . . Let no one add anything to them or take anything away from them."[14]

More discussions on the canon would continue, but by this time a general consensus had been reached. The Bible had grown in relative proportion to its divine revelation—gradually—and its books likewise had gradually assumed the roles which their inherent authority demanded.

Related Observations

It is sometimes said that the line of demarcation between the New Testament books and other Christian writings was not always clear, that scarcely any distinction was made between the two. But early Christians were not as uncritical or naive about these matters as they are often made out to be. Jesus and his apostles warned about false prophets, and at least some congregations were commended for holding their ground (Rev. 2:2; 1 John 4:4). The church that was instructed not to believe every spirit (cf. 1 John 4:1) certainly had some capacity for discerning divine authority. But with the rapid growth of Christianity, it was inevitable that in some quarters of the church various Christian writings would be received differently.

There was a great deal of discussion about certain books, and the New Testament canon is better because of such discussions. Several of our New Testament books, at least for a while, were included among the "disputed" books. But these books were questioned not because they taught a different gospel but, especially in several instances, because they were not well known and widely circulated in the church. James, 2 and 3 John, and perhaps others, are to be included in this group.

As for other Christian writings, a number of them were circulating among Christians. Especially important among these were the Epistle of Barnabas and the Shepherd of Hermas. The first was written probably in the first part of the second century by someone other than the New Testament Barnabas. The second is an allegory from about the same time, written by a member of the church at Rome called Hermas. Yet neither of these books were above suspicion, nor were they generally received on a par with the acknowledged apostolic writings. In the case of the Shepherd of Hermas, for example, the above mentioned Muratorian Fragment states that it could be read in public worship but that it was not to be counted among the prophets or apostolic writings.

The restriction concerning the Shepherd of Hermas serves to illustrate the significant principle that some books could be read for edification in public worship which were not at the time regarded as possessing divine authority. In this category fall the Shepherd of Hermas and possibly the Epistle of Barnabas. These and a few others were sometimes included in the early manuscripts, but according to the Muratorian Fragment it is a mistake to think that every book that was read in the churches was necessarily accorded apostolic standing.

Even today in public assemblies, as purposes of teaching and edification may demand, selections from secular works are sometimes read. It was no different in the days of the early church, nor is there sufficient reason to think the early church was less discerning in distinguishing between inspired and noninspired materials.

In the final analysis, canon is not something that once and for all can be proved. The study of canon is a study of history, and each generation must give itself to that study. This is but another reason why we should try to learn more about the Bible and how it has come down to us.

Summary

The word "canon" as used in this study refers to the list of books which are acknowledged as being divinely inspired and are included in the Bible. The formation of the canon was a gradual process, just as the books themselves came into being gradually. By the time of our Lord it is evident that the Old Testament canon was well defined; a clear distinction is maintained between "Scripture" and non-Scripture. Evidence as to the exact books of Old Testament Scripture is furnished by the numerous quotations found in the New Testament of the Old Testament and from other early Christian and non-Christian sources.

As to the New Testament books, not long after they were written, they were being read regularly in the church assemblies. They were held in high esteem by early Christians. The words of Jesus and his apostles were no less authoritative than the Old Testament. In this way the New Testament canon gradually took shape. By the close of the second century its essentials had been largely determined, and by the next century or two the New Testament books as they are known today constituted the supreme authority for the primitive church.

In conclusion, it is important to emphasize that no church council *made* the canon of Scripture. No church by its decrees gave to or pronounced on the books of the Bible their infallibility. The Bible owes its authority to no individual or group. The church does not control the canon, but the canon controls the church. Although divine authority was attributed to the New Testament books by the later church, this authority was not derived from the church but was inherent in the books themselves. As a child identifies its mother, the later church *identified* the books which it regarded as having unique authority.

For Discussion

1. What is meant by the canon of the Scriptures? Distinguish between a book's canonicity and its authority. Is authority dependent on canonicity or canonicity dependent on authority?
2. Is there any information in the New Testament which has bearing on the Old Testament canon? What statement of Jesus indicates which books were included in the Old Testament of his day? Did his Old Testament differ from ours?
3. What other evidence is there for the Old Testament canon? How is it that the twenty-two books of the Jews equal our thirty-nine books?
4. Describe briefly the first stages in the formation of a New Testament canon.
5. Name and discuss some of the early lists of New Testament books. Is it natural to expect some differences in the early lists? Why?
6. Explain why a decision of a church council cannot make certain books infallible. Does the church control the canon of Scripture?

15

The Apocryphal Books

oday there is very little discussion concerning which books rightfully belong in the Bible. The canon of the Holy Scriptures is settled. But the question of the canon has been decided differently in different parts of Christendom. Catholicism and Protestantism are united in their acceptance of the twenty-seven books of the New Testament, but concerning the books of the Old Testament this is not the case. The Roman Catholic Bible contains several additional books in its Old Testament section that are not found in most Protestant Bibles. These extra books are generally referred to as the "Apocrypha."

The word *apocrypha* has come into the English language from the Greek and basically means "hidden." It was used very early in the sense of "secretive" or "concealed" but was also used in reference to a book whose origin was doubtful or unknown. Eventually the word took on the meaning of "noncanonical" and thus for centuries the noncanonical books have been known as apocryphal books. Yet in Protestant circles "the Apocrypha" is the normal designation for those extra books which are found in the Catholic Old Testament. On the other hand, Roman Catholics use the terms "protocanonical" and "deuterocanonical," holding a distinction between a first or original canon (Greek *protos*, meaning "first") and a secondary canon (Greek *deuteros*, meaning "second"). Instead of "apocrypha" the Roman Catholic term is "deuterocanonical," acknowledging that these questioned books were not originally a part of the canon but were accepted later.

Apocryphal Books of the Old Testament

Strictly speaking, it might be better to refer to these books as the Old Testament Apocrypha, since there are New Testament apocryphal writings as well. The Old Testament Apocrypha includes either fourteen or fifteen books, depending on the method of counting, which were written in the period of 300 B.C. to A.D. 100. In recent years the Apocrypha has appeared in a number of special editions of the English Bible, but these sometimes differ in which books are included and in what order. Given below is a list of the books that are traditionally included in the Apocrypha.

1. The First Book of Esdras (also known as Third Esdras)
2. The Second Book of Esdras (also known as Fourth Esdras)
3. Tobit
4. Judith
5. The Additions to the Book of Esther
6. The Wisdom of Solomon
7. Ecclesiasticus, or the Wisdom of Jesus the Son of Sirach
8. Baruch
9. The Letter of Jeremiah (This letter is sometimes incorporated as the last chapter of Baruch. When this is done, the number of books is fourteen instead of fifteen.)
10. The Prayer of Azariah and the Song of the Three Young Men
11. Susanna
12. Bel and the Dragon
13. The Prayer of Manasseh
14. The First Book of Maccabees
15. The Second Book of Maccabees

Three of these fifteen books (1 and 2 Esdras and the Prayer
of Manasseh) are not considered canonical by the Roman
Catholic Church. In Catholic Bibles the remaining twelve are
interspersed among and attached to the undisputed thirty-nine
books of the Old Testament: Tobit, Judith, Wisdom of Solomon,
Ecclesiasticus, Baruch with the letter of Jeremiah, and 1 and
2 Maccabees, all of which are arranged separately; the Additions to Esther are naturally joined to Esther; and appended
to the Book of Daniel are the Prayer of Azariah and the Song
of the Three Young Men (added after Dan. 3:23), Susanna, and
Bel and the Dragon. (First and Second Esdras of the Catholic
Bible are not the same as the 1 and 2 Esdras in the above list
but are different designations for our books Ezra and Nehemiah.) Since several of the apocryphal writings are combined
with canonical books, the Catholic Bible numbers altogether
forty-six books in its Old Testament. Non-Catholic editions of
the English Bible since 1535, including early editions of the
familiar King James Version, separate these apocryphal books
from the canonical Old Testament.

Contents of These Books

The Old Testament Apocrypha covers a broad range of subjects and represents different varieties of literary form. For
purposes of convenience they may be classified under the following divisions:

1. Historical—1 Esdras, 1 and 2 Maccabees.
2. Legendary—Tobit, Judith, Additions to Esther, Additions
   to Daniel (Prayer of Azariah and Song of the Three Young
   Men, Susanna, and Bel and the Dragon).
3. Prophetic—Baruch, Letter of Jeremiah, 2 Esdras.
4. Ethical/Devotional—Ecclesiasticus, Wisdom of Solomon,
   Prayer of Manasseh.

Something of the character of these writings will now be
mentioned.

1. Historical. First Esdras is an ill-arranged collection of much of the material found in the canonical Ezra (Esdras is a Greek form of Ezra) and includes legendary accounts which are not supported by the books of 1 and 2 Chronicles, Ezra, and Nehemiah. It is also known as the "Greek Ezra" in contrast to the "Hebrew Ezra" (the canonical Ezra). First Maccabees is an important source of information on Jewish history during the second century B.C. The book derives its name from Maccabeus, the nickname of Judas who led the Jews in revolt against Syrian oppression. It was written near the close of the second century B.C. Second Maccabees concerns the same general period but is not as historically reliable as 1 Maccabees.

2. Legendary. The Book of Tobit was written about 200 B.C. It tells the story of a religious Israelite named Tobit who was carried as a captive to Nineveh by the Assyrians. Its purpose is to encourage the keeping of the Law, yet the fictitious character of its tales detracts from its usefulness. The Book of Judith is likewise to be classified as fiction. Judith is the name of a Jewish widow who successfully charms and kills the leader of an enemy army, thus delivering her city and people from impending destruction. This story of heroism was perhaps composed during the time of the Maccabean revolt, or a little later, to incite a patriotic spirit against Jewish foes.

The Additions to Esther are expansions of the canonical Esther which were probably handed down through the centuries by oral tradition. The Additions to Daniel contain tales and legends which originated probably not much earlier than 100 B.C. and form no part of the genuine text of Daniel.

3. Prophetic. Baruch purports to come from the hand of Jeremiah's friend of that name. The contents of the book make this claim impossible and show that it goes back to about the beginning of the Christian era. The Letter of Jeremiah, which for no good reason is often appended to Baruch, is a tract on the vanities of idolatry. Though dating as early as 300 B.C., it could not have been written by the prophet Jeremiah. Second Esdras is an apocalyptic work (Greek *apocalypsis,* meaning "revelation") that professes to be a revelation given in a series

of visions to Ezra. Whether written by one or more authors, it is usually dated about A.D. 100. It is of such inferior quality that it is unquestionably noncanonical.

4. Ethical/Devotional. Ecclesiasticus, or the Wisdom of Jesus the Son of Sirach, is one of the chief works of the Apocrypha. It was written by a Palestinian Jew about 200 B.C. in a style similar to the wise sayings of the Book of Proverbs. The Wisdom of Solomon is a book of ancient Jewish philosophy. It is evidently to be traced back to the city of Alexandria and to the first century A.D. The Prayer of Manasseh, written perhaps in the second century B.C., is a prayer put in the mouth of King Manasseh after he was taken captive in Babylon.[1]

Why These Books Are Rejected

A brief survey of these books has indicated something of what they are like. Some of the books of the Apocrypha, such as 1 Maccabees and Ecclesiasticus, are truly worthwhile. Other books likewise are valuable. For example, the Prayer of Manasseh, though not at all from Manasseh, nevertheless is a beautiful prayer of repentance. The question here, however, concerns not the usefulness of these books but their place in relation to the authoritative Scriptures. Should they be received as Scripture or rejected? And if they are to be rejected, on what grounds? Are there really good reasons why they should not be accepted as divinely authoritative?

There are many valid reasons why the Apocrypha cannot bear acceptance as Holy Scripture.

1. These books were never included in the Hebrew canon of the Old Testament. Josephus, it will be recalled, expressly limited the Hebrew canon to twenty-two books, which are the exact equivalent to the thirty-nine books of our Old Testament. Josephus knew of other Jewish writings down to his time, but he did not regard them as having equal authority with the canonical works. So the apocryphal books were never received by the Jews as God-given Scripture. This takes on its full significance when it is remembered that the Old Testament

is a Jewish collection of Jewish history and law. There is no evidence that the Apocrypha was ever accepted by any Jewish community, either in or outside the land of Palestine.

2. These books, as far as the evidence goes, were never accepted as canonical by Jesus and his apostles. In chapter 13 we saw that the Old Testament which Jesus knew is our Old Testament today. Jesus' Old Testament was the Hebrew Old Testament, and the Hebrew Old Testament has never included these apocryphal writings. The apostles in their preaching mention many Old Testament events, but they never refer to any incidents or characters of the Apocrypha. The New Testament writers quote from practically all of the Old Testament books but nowhere quote from any of the Apocrypha. The canon of the Old Testament accepted by Jesus and his apostles should be sufficient for Christians today.

3. These books were not accepted as Scripture by such Jewish writers of the first century as Philo and Josephus; by the Jewish council at Jamnia (c. A.D. 90); and by such eminent Christian writers as Origen and Jerome.[2] About A.D. 400 the great scholar Jerome, whose translation of the Latin Vulgate remains the basis of the official Roman Catholic Bible, strongly maintained that these books were apocryphal and were not to be included in the canon of Scripture.

4. These books do not evidence intrinsic qualities of inspiration. Great portions of these books are obviously legendary and fictitious. Often they contain historical, chronological, and geographical errors. In Judith, for example, Holofernes is described as being the general of "Nebuchadnezzar who ruled over the Assyrians in the great city of Nineveh" (1:1). Actually, Holofernes was a Persian general, and, of course, Nebuchadnezzar was king of the Babylonians in Babylon. Judith has other historical mistakes as well, which sometimes have been defended.[3] Even in the unlikely case that these mistakes can be justified, there is the greater problem of the character of Judith herself. By her use of flattery and lies, even praying that God might "use the deceit upon [her] lips" (9:10), the heroine of the story (Judith) ends up enforcing the principle of doing evil that good may come.

Historical inaccuracies are spread through other books of the Apocrypha. First Maccabees includes historical slips, and 2 Maccabees certainly is not straightforward history. Tobit, like Judith, records a number of errors. But the trouble with so many books of the Apocrypha is that they abound with exaggerated exploits, fanciful stories, and just plain fiction. Sometimes they are self-contradictory, and sometimes they contradict the canonical Scriptures. Baruch, for instance, pretends to have been written by Jeremiah's companion during the Babylonian captivity but actually was written much later.

5. These books have been shrouded with continual uncertainty. Since they were not regarded as authoritative by the Jews, they had to gain their recognition elsewhere. This recognition came from some segments of the Greek-speaking church, with the result that eventually these books became incorporated into the Greek and Latin Bibles. But there is no evidence that the Septuagint (the Greek translation of the Old Testament) ever had a fixed or closed canon of books. No two early Greek manuscripts agree as to which books are to be included in the Septuagint, and not all of those included in the Septuagint are accepted by the Roman Catholic Church. The Septuagint itself is a witness against one book of the Apocrypha, 2 Esdras, since it is found in no manuscript of the Septuagint.

6. These books cannot be maintained on a compromise basis. The Church of England gives to the Apocrypha a semicanonical status: they may be read in public worship "for example of life and instruction of manners" but not in order "to establish any doctrine."[4] This position assumes that the Apocrypha at times may add to or conflict with the established teachings of the canonical Scriptures. If this is true, then the Apocrypha should not be a part of the public readings in worship, for what is read regularly in worship tends to be authoritative for the congregation. To allow the apocryphal books to be read in worship is a strange way to show their subordinate rank.

7. Objections to these books cannot be overruled by dictatorial authority. On 8 April 1546 in the fourth session of the Council of Trent, the Roman Catholic Church pronounced the Old Testament Apocrypha (except 1 and 2 Esdras, and the Prayer

of Manasseh) as authoritative and canonical Scripture. This was done even though in different periods of its own history officials of the Roman Church had been outspoken against the Apocrypha as Scripture. At that time the Council also decreed that the Latin Vulgate only was to be regarded as authentic Scripture and that "holy Mother Church" alone maintained the right to give the true interpretation of Scripture. But this action was not unnatural for a religious body whose whole structure is framed according to traditions and whose faith is derived equally as much from the interpretations of the church as from the Scriptures. Indeed, according to the Council of Trent, the Scriptures are and mean what the church says. Yet Rome, which in such matters claims infallibility, cannot make the fallible Apocrypha infallible.

A Frequent Question

If the Apocrypha is to be rejected, and if the New Testament writers do not quote from it, sometimes questions are raised about references made in the Book of Jude to noncanonical literature. These verses are Jude 9 and 14–15, concerning which only brief comments can be made.

Jude 9 supposedly alludes to a work called the Assumption of Moses. This survives only in fragments, but the extant fragments do not have the incident referred to in Jude. Jude 14–15 is from an apocalyptic book known as 1 Enoch.[5] There are several possible explanations for these passages, but it is nothing especially unusual that Jude makes use of extra-Biblical materials. The Apostle Paul does this (2 Tim. 3:8) and even calls one of the Greek poets a "prophet" (Titus 1:12). Of course, Paul did not believe that the poet was a prophet like Isaiah or Jeremiah. So when Jude writes against false teachers, whether he refers to a traditional story about the body of Moses (v. 9) or to a "prophecy" of Enoch (vv. 14–15), he may be doing no more than we often do. He may be speaking to his audience illustratively, using the writings that were so familiar to his readers and to his opponents.[6]

The Apocryphal Books of the New Testament

The Old Testament Apocrypha is usually thought of when one mentions the apocryphal books. Nevertheless, there are other apocryphal writings, many of which are known as the New Testament Apocrypha. The New Testament Apocrypha superficially tries to imitate the kinds of books in the New Testament and thus includes a variety of literary types: Gospels, Acts, Epistles, and Apocalypses. Dating from the second century and later, these books were written under assumed names: the Gospel of Peter, the Protevangelium (meaning "first gospel") of James, the Gospel of Bartholomew, the Infancy Story of Thomas, the Acts of Peter, the Acts of John, the Acts of Paul—on and on it goes.[7] Such works, to say the least, present highly fanciful stories of Jesus during his early years or while he was in the tomb or after his resurrection; imaginative tales about the missionary activities of the apostles; letters supposedly written by the apostles; and apocalypses of Peter and others that pretend to reveal the future.

Anyone who has doubts about the New Testament canon should take the time to read some of the New Testament Apocrypha. Here are a few examples of what one may find: (1) Infancy Story of Thomas. When a child bumps his shoulder, Jesus strikes him dead. (2) Gospel of Peter. Three men come out of Jesus' tomb, with a cross following them; the head of two of them reaches to heaven, the head of the other overpasses the heavens. (3) Protevangelium of James. Mary is brought up in the temple, dedicated as a virgin from the age of three. (4) Acts of John. John, on finding bedbugs in his bed at an inn, commands the bugs to leave and behave themselves. (5) Acts of Paul. Paul baptizes a lion, who later spares him from death in the amphitheater at Ephesus.

After reading such tales, many of us will want to hurry back to our New Testaments and once again appreciate them both for what they say and what they do not say. At the same time we should be grateful that the early church did distinguish between these apocryphal books and those that comprise the New Testament.

The writings of the Apostolic Fathers (A.D. 95–155) are not to be classified as New Testament Apocrypha. They are simply letters of edification and encouragement written by ordinary Christians; they do not profess apostolic wisdom and authority. These writings, along with the apocryphal books, are sometimes erroneously described as "the lost books of the Bible," a sensational and misleading title because these books were never a part of the Bible.

Summary

The word "apocrypha" may be used with equal application to the noncanonical books of the Old and New Testaments. Generally speaking, however, it is the common designation for a special group of fourteen or fifteen books, most of which are included in the Old Testament of the Roman Catholic Bible. The Apocrypha may be divided into four groups: (1) historical, (2) legendary, (3) prophetic, and (4) ethical/devotional. These books are useful but should not be regarded as Scripture for the following reasons:

1. They were never included in the Hebrew Old Testament.
2. They were never accepted as canonical by Jesus and his apostles.
3. They were not accepted by early Jewish and Christian writers.
4. They do not evidence intrinsic qualities of inspiration.
5. They have been shrouded with continual uncertainty.
6. They cannot be maintained on a compromise basis.
7. Objections to them cannot be overruled by dictatorial authority.

The apocryphal books, whether associated with the Old or New Testaments, are rightfully rejected from our Bible.

For Discussion

1. What is the basic meaning of the word "apocrypha"? How is it generally used?
2. Review the list of the Apocryphal books. How many are there? Which two books are sometimes joined together and thus affect the total number of books?
3. As to the subject matter, how may the books of the Apocrypha be divided?
4. What three books of the Apocrypha are not included in the Roman Catholic Bible?
5. What are some of the values of the Apocrypha?
6. What seven reasons stand opposed to receiving the Apocrypha as Scripture? Is each reason valid?
7. Why should the New Testament Apocrypha not be included in the New Testament?

16

The English Bible to 1611

nother phase of the Bible's transmission lies in the history of English translations. Christianity made its entrance into Britain no later than the third century, but at that time the Scriptures were not available in translation. The Latin language was then assuming dominance in the West as the language of the learned, which meant that the early Bibles in England were not in English but Latin. Yet it was in England, so long deprived of the Living Word, where the battle was fought and won for the right of the common man to have his Bible in his own language.

The Earliest English Versions

The beginnings of the English Bible go back to the middle of the seventh century. An unlearned laborer by the name of Caedmon is reported to have arranged in verse form stories of the Bible on subjects ranging from the creation to the work of the apostles. Although these verses were not really translations, they mark the first known attempt to put the Bible accounts in the native Anglo-Saxon. The next generation saw the first actual translation of any part of the Bible in English. The translation was the work of Aldhelm (d. 709), and the portion of Scripture translated was the Book of Psalms. A little later the venerable Bede (d. 735) is said to have finished in the last hours of his life a translation of the Gospel of John, but of his translation nothing has been preserved. Toward the close of the ninth century King Alfred (d. 901) led his people in a religious reform that resulted in a translation of the Psalms and other sections of Scripture. In the tenth century Abbot Aelfric translated additional portions of the Old Testament. Altogether the Old English versions that have survived include the Pentateuch, some historical books of the Old Testament, the Psalms, and the Gospels.

The Norman Conquest in 1066 brought about many changes in England. Chief among these was a modification of the language, now known as Middle English. It was not until the thirteenth and fourteenth centuries before parts of the Bible were put in English, and here the names of William of Shoreham and Richard Rolle stand out. It was their work on the Psalms in the first half of the fourteenth century that planted the seed of a struggle which was to last for two centuries in putting the Bible in the hands of the common people.

Wycliffe

A memorable name in the story of the English Bible is John Wycliffe. The England that he knew most of his life (1330–1384) was full of faction and unrest, much of which had been brought on by the Roman pope's excessive demands for money. An Oxford scholar and teacher, Wycliffe emerged in the controversy over papal oppression as the champion of the people. Wycliffe's first written work was in defense of Parliament in 1366 for its refusal to turn over money claimed by the pope. It was this uncompromising spirit that shortly afterward urged him on in the fight for social and religious reforms. So Wycliffe and his associates called England to the great spiritual revival of the fourteenth century.

Wycliffe had the peculiar idea that the common man was worth something. "No man," he said, "was so rude a scholar but that he might learn the words of the Gospel according to his simplicity."[1] In this belief, during the last years of his life and with the assistance of some of his students, Wycliffe undertook a translation of the Scriptures from the Latin into the English tongue. This work was completed in about 1382, the first English translation of the complete Bible.

No one knows how much of the translation Wycliffe did himself, perhaps some of it, perhaps none of it at all. Yet we refer to the translation as the Wycliffe version, for it was due to his scholarship and under his influence that the historic project was accomplished. In about 1388 an anonymous revision of Wycliffe's Bible appeared, translated perhaps by John Purvey, who was one of the Lollards. The Lollards were the followers of Wycliffe, "poor priests" who went out among the people and taught the gospel in a language they could understand. Lollardy and Wycliffe's Bible were to prepare the way in England for the Reformation of the sixteenth century.

Tyndale

The true father of the English Bible is William Tyndale. The story of Tyndale and his unrelenting efforts to put the Bible in the hands of the people is a story of triumph mingled with tears. In the year 1511 the monk-scholar Erasmus came to Cambridge as professor of Greek. Several years later young Tyndale also came to Cambridge, probably to study Greek and certainly to study the Scriptures more at leisure. Under the influence of his training received at Cambridge, and earlier at Oxford, Tyndale's ambition to give to the English people a translation of the Bible based not on Latin but the original Greek and Hebrew became his chief end in life. To an opponent he once said, "If God spare my life, ere many years I will cause a boy that driveth the plow shall know more of the Scripture than thou doest."[2] Consciously or unconsciously he was reflecting a similar conviction of Erasmus: "I would to God the plowman would sing a text of the scripture at his plow, and the weaver at his loom with this would drive away the tediousness of time.

(176)

Courtesy of the British and Foreign Bible Society, London, England

Portrait of William Tyndale.

I would that the wayfaring man with this pastime would expel the weariness of his journey."[3]

Erasmus had issued in 1516 the first printed New Testament in Greek, and Tyndale had set out to translate it. In 1524 Tyndale had to leave England after finding out "that there was no place to do it [translate the New Testament] in all of England."[4] The following year in Germany, perhaps in Hamburg, his translation was completed, and he sought to have it printed in Cologne.

By now Tyndale's efforts at translation associated him with the Reformer Martin Luther, who had recently finished a translation in German. Thus the many enemies of the Reformation and of Luther were likewise enemies of Tyndale. Accordingly, Tyndale had to flee from Cologne with the sheets of his partially printed New Testament. In another German city, Worms, which was disposed favorably to the Reformation, the printing of his New Testament was completed. Early in 1526 the first copies were smuggled into England and bought with enthusiasm. Officials of the Roman Church condemned the translation. Copies were obtained and burned in public ceremony. Money was subscribed to buy incoming copies. But all this opposition could not wipe out a movement that was making itself felt around the world.

In the meantime Tyndale had taken up his work of translating the Old Testament from Hebrew. By 1530 he had translated and published the Pentateuch. Then came Jonah (1531), a revised Genesis (1534), and two additional editions of his New Testament (1534–35). By now his translations, although not welcomed, were not as violently opposed by official England, and it appeared as though the long-fought contest might turn in his favor. But many Romanists were still determined to stamp out heresy. In 1535 Tyndale was betrayed, Judas-like, and was imprisoned in Vilvorde Castle, near Brussels.

In the years previous to his confinement, Tyndale was an exiled, hunted man. In 1531 he spoke of his deprivations: "my pains . . . my poverty . . . my exile out of my natural country, and bitter absence from my friends . . . my hunger, my thirst, my cold, the great danger wherewith I am everywhere compassed, and . . . innumerable other hard and sharp fightings which I endure. . . ."[5] The words were truly an autobiography of his last years.

Tyndale's sacrifice for his cause has long been appreciated, but it is doubtful if many today know how direct and pervasive his influence was on the English Bible. It was Tyndale who established its tone, that the Bible should not be in the language of scholars but in the spoken language of the people. Tyndale used the word "congregation" instead of "church," "love" instead of "charity," "repentance" instead of "penance," and so forth. He coined such words as "Passover," "scapegoat," "mercy seat," and "long-suffering."

Many expressions of Tyndale are also unforgettable, cherished by countless readers of the English Bible: "the kingdom of heaven is at hand" (Matt. 3:2); "the pinnacle of the temple" (Matt. 4:5); "the salt of the earth" (Matt. 5:13); "daily bread" (Matt. 6:11); "Consider the lilies of the field, how they grow" (Matt. 6:28); "meek and lowly in heart" (Matt. 11:29); "shepherds abiding in the field" (Luke 2:8); "eat, drink, and be merry" (Luke 12:19); "fatted calf" (Luke 15:23); "only begotten son" (John 1:14, 18);[6] "in my Father's house are many mansions" (John 14:2); "in whom we live and move and have our being" (Acts 17:28); "God forbid" (Rom. 3:4); "sounding brass" and "tinkling cymbal" (1 Cor. 13:1); "in the twinkling of an eye" (1 Cor. 15:52); "singing and making melody" (Eph. 5:19); "office of a bishop" (1 Tim. 3:1); "the pleasures of sin for a season" (Heb. 11:25); "an advocate with the Father" (1 John 2:1); and "Behold, I stand at the door and knock" (Rev. 3:20).

The above is a short list of quotations from the 1534 edition of Tyndale's New Testament, except the spelling has been modernized. It is noteworthy that these expressions could have been translated differently from the Greek text, yet because Tyndale had such an ear for the English language, these phrases live on.

Tyndale's work was not flawless. Many of his renderings needed the corrections made in later translations, but he unquestionably achieved what he sought: a translation that could be understood even by the boy at the plow. His dedication, his good heart, and his devotion to his task stand out over the centuries. This is well illustrated by several sentences in his preface to his 1534 New Testament, entitled "W. T. unto the Reader."

> Moreover, I take God (which alone seeth the heart) to record to my conscience, beseeching him that my part be not in the blood of Christ, if I wrote of all that I have written through out all my book, ought of an evil purpose, of envy or malice to any man, or to stir up any false doctrine or opinion in the church of Christ, or to be author of any sect, or to draw away disciples after me. . . . Also, my part be not in Christ, if mine heart be not to follow and live according as I teach. . . .
>
> As concerning all I have translated or other wise written, I beseech all men to read it for that purpose I wrote it: even to

bring them to the knowledge of the scripture. And as far as the scripture approveth it, so far to allow it, and if in any place the word of god disallow it, there to refuse it, as I do before our saviour Christ and his congregation. . . .

Steadfastly defending these principles, unbending to the end, on an October morning in 1536, Tyndale went to the stake. He was strangled and burned, crying out, "Lord, open the king of England's eyes."

Other Sixteenth-Century Translations

Tyndale died, but he had "lighted such a candle, by God's grace, in England, as should never be put out."[7] Even before his death the tide had begun to change. Admirers of Tyndale like to think that while he was in prison he heard about the publication in England (1535) of a Bible partly based on his own. This Bible was that of Miles Coverdale, a former friend and associate of Tyndale. Coverdale was not the scholar that Tyndale was, but his translation is significant because it was the first in England to circulate without official hindrance.

A flood of translations and revisions was to follow. Matthew's Bible, actually the work of Tyndale's friend John Rogers, appeared in 1537. It was a combined edition of both Tyndale and Coverdale. Taverner's Bible of 1539 was an independent revision of Matthew's Bible, and its chief contribution has to do with a number of improved renderings in the New Testament.

In the same year another revision of Matthew's Bible came out, known as the Great Bible. Edited by Coverdale, it was the first of the English Bibles authorized to be read in the churches. It was the wish of Henry VIII that it go abroad among the people, and in keeping with the king's wish, a copy of the Great Bible was placed in every church in the land.[8] People flocked eagerly to the churches to see the Bibles which had been set up for reading, and at times the preachers complained because the people chose rather to hear the reading of the Bible than to listen to their sermons. Tyndale's dying prayer at last had been answered: the Lord had opened the king of England's eyes.

Another Bible, however, was destined to be the most popular Bible of the century. It was the Geneva Bible of 1560, so called because it was printed in Geneva. Under Queen Mary persecution of non-Catholics had begun again, and many English citizens had been driven from England. In Geneva they found a safe haven, where English scholars translated the New Testament by 1557, which was followed by the complete Bible three years later.

Produced in legible type, in small form, with accompanying commentary and illustrations, the Geneva Bible became the Bible for the family just as the Great Bible was the Bible for the church. The Geneva Bible was the first translation to print each verse as a paragraph and to put words in italics not represented in the original texts. It is sometimes called the "Breeches Bible" because it says that Adam and Eve "sewed figge tree leaves together, and made themselves breeches" (Gen. 3:7).

The Geneva Bible went through some 140 editions (in Bible or New Testament) and continued its popular acceptance even after the appearance of the King James Version. It was the Bible used by Shakespeare in his later plays; it was the Bible of the Jamestown settlement in Virginia; it was the Bible brought to Plymouth on the Mayflower. And it was a Bible, with its improved Hebrew and Greek scholarship, that was an intermediate step between Tyndale and the King James Version.

But the Geneva Bible was not popular with the English church officials. Its commentary presented the views of John Calvin and the Reformation. Therefore, a revision of the Great Bible was begun by the English clergy, and when completed in 1568, it was known as the Bishops' Bible. Four years later a second edition appeared, but the Bishops' Bible neither measured up to the scholarship nor attained to the popularity of the Geneva Bible.

The zeal of Protestant revisions and editions eventually forced into being a Roman Catholic translation of the Bible. An edition of the New Testament was produced in 1582 at the English college of Rheims, and in 1609–10 the college at Douai issued a translation of the Old Testament. The Rheims-Douai translation was thus the first Roman Catholic edition of the English Bible. It was translated, however, not from the original languages of Scripture but from the Latin Vulgate.

The King James Version

The Authorized Version of 1611, better known as the King James Version, did what its many predecessors were unable to do—provide a translation for public and private use which was satisfactory to all. In 1604 King James summoned a meeting of representatives of diverse religious groups to discuss the question of religious toleration. At this gathering, known as the Hampton Court Conference, Dr. John Reynolds of Oxford raised the possibility of a new translation. The king welcomed the suggestion and soon was working out the necessary procedures for its realization.

James himself, it seems, laid down the main requirements which were to be followed, one of the chief rules being there were to be no notes of comment except what was essential in translating the text. The Geneva Bible was distinctively one-sided in its comments, and James knew that the way to satisfy all parties was to withhold from the margins the private viewpoint of any one party. Such provisions for the new translation were probably the wisest thing that the otherwise unwise king ever did.[9]

By 1607, or perhaps earlier, the work of the translators had formally begun. Their task was not to make a new translation but to revise the 1602 edition of the Bishops' Bible. About forty-eight choice Greek and Hebrew scholars were selected and divided into six working companies, two at Westminster, two at Oxford, and two at Cambridge. Each company, restricted in its labors by detailed instructions, was assigned selected books to be translated, and the work of each company was sent to and reviewed by the other companies. Appointed delegates of each company smoothed out the difficult spots. In this way the translation was the product of no individual or group but of the reviewers as a whole.

The work of revision continued for two years and nine months (perhaps longer), after which it was turned over to the printers. It was in 1611, seven years after the convening of the Hampton Court Conference, that the first copies of the new version came from the press. It was dedicated to the king, and on its title page were the words "Appointed to be read in Churches." Accompanying it was a truly great preface entitled "The Translators to the Reader," in which the translators sought to justify their efforts against the many voices of critics who felt that their old Bibles were good enough. It is a pity that this preface, which is not to be confused with the dedication note, is no longer printed in many editions of the King James Bible. It is timely even today, and especially so for those who are always opposing new translations.[10]

The King James translation has passed through many editions and has been modernized considerably over the years. In 1613 a new edition was issued which contained more than four hundred variations from the original printing.[11] Countless other emendations have taken place through the centuries of its existence, so many changes that the King James reader of today would be startled by the appearance of the 1611 edition.

Appointed for use in public worship, the King James immediately displaced the Bishops' Bible in the churches, but in private use the new translation received stiff competition from the popular Geneva Bible. Within a few decades, however, it had established itself as the translation for English-speaking people around the world.

Reasons for its supremacy are not hard to find. First, Greek and Hebrew scholarship had made tremendous strides during the seventy-five years that had elapsed since the time of Tyndale. Study of the Biblical languages had ceased during the Middle Ages and had been revived only recently when Tyndale made his first translation. The sixteenth century, following Tyndale, was marked by such a resurgence of interest in the Biblical languages that, when it came time for King James to constitute his revision committee, he could look in many directions for men of capable and sound scholarship. Second, literary scholarship and learning in general at this time were at a high. It was the period of Elizabethan prose and poetry, the age in which Spenser and Shakespeare flowered. Under these influences the revisers were able to produce a translation carefully framed in a classic English style. Third, the revision was made at an opportune time. A good English translation was needed, and the translators were able to profit from both the excellencies and the shortcomings of previous translations. Fourth, the revision was the work of no one man or party. England had been torn by religious factions, and partisan translations could not supply the remedy. A translation that endures can represent no single viewpoint, and that the King James Version has lasted for several centuries is a tribute to its deliberate impartiality.

Summary

The story of the English Bible is as interesting as the story of a mighty nation. John Wycliffe was the first man to give to the English people a translation that could be read in their native tongue. Wycliffe's translation, however, was based on the Latin Vulgate. It was William Tyndale who was the first to envision and bring into reality an English translation based on the original Greek and Hebrew languages. Erasmus had greatly accelerated Tyndale's ambition by having already published the New Testament in Greek. Tyndale's New Testament was first printed in 1525 and went through several editions, but Tyndale suffered martyrdom before he was able to complete his work on the Old Testament. Many translations followed Tyndale's: Coverdale's (1535), Matthew's Bible (1537), Taverner's (1539), the Great Bible (1539), the Geneva Bible (1560), the Bishops' Bible (1568), and the Authorized Version (1611). Tyndale's translation was the first based on the Greek and Hebrew texts, and it was his labors which opened the way for other translations. How appropriate it is that more than 80 percent of Tyndale's translation is preserved today in the

King James Version. William Tyndale is truly the father of the
English Bible.

For Discussion

1. When did the Wycliffe translation first appear? Why was
   it so long before the English people had a translation in
   their own tongue?
2. Relate the high points in the story of Tyndale's translation of the New Testament. In what year did Tyndale fin-
   ish his New Testament translation? Where was it printed
   and how did it get to England? Wycliffe's translation had
   been based on the Latin. Upon what did Tyndale base his
   translation?
3. What were the translations that immediately followed
   Tyndale's and when were they published? Which Bible
   was the first to be authorized for use in the churches?
4. Why was the Geneva Bible so popular? How was it different from the Bishops' Bible of 1568?
5. What events led to the appearance of the King James Bible?
   Was the King James Version a revision or a completely new
   translation? How many scholars were engaged in the work
   of translation? How long did they work?
6. For what reasons was the King James Version superior
   to its predecessors?

17

Recent Translations
of the English Bible

he publication of the King James Version in 1611 was an epoch-making event in the history of the English Bible. Itself a revision, it was the climax of various translations and revisions. For many years it maintained an unquestioned supremacy, a supremacy so great that it has caused many people to regard it as the final word on Bible translation. But no translation is ever final. Because translators are human beings, there will always be room for improvements of translations. No translator can transcend his own time. He can only work in light of the knowledge of his day, with materials available to him, and put his translation in words spoken by his generation.

Weaknesses of the King James

Several weaknesses of the King James made more recent revisions necessary.

1. The King James Version rests on an inadequate textual base. This is especially true with reference to the Greek text for the New Testament. The text underlying the King James was essentially a medieval text that contained a number of scribal

mistakes that had accumulated through the years. Most of these textual variations were small in significance and did not materially affect the Bible message, but others deserved no place in the Holy Scriptures. An example of this, as we have seen, is 1 John 5:7 (see chapter 9). The revisers of 1611 are not at fault here. They simply did not have at their disposal the many manuscripts that are now known. It is important to remember that three of the most valuable witnesses on the New Testament text (the Vatican, the Sinaitic, and the Alexandrian Manuscripts) were not available when the King James translation was made. Nor were many other important manuscripts accessible to the translators, including the very early papyrus documents. All of this means the King James is a translation of an inferior Greek text, and therefore a revision of it based on earlier manuscripts was imperative.

2. The King James Version contains many archaic words whose meanings are either obscure or misleading. Some obsolete expressions are still intelligible, although they are extremely cumbersome and distracting to the modern reader: "howbeit," "holden," "peradventure," "because that," "for that," "thee," "thou," "thy," "thine," and many others. At other times, however, the King James uses words that in the seventeenth century meant something different than they do today. The word "allege" was used for "prove," "communicate" for "share," "suffer" for "allow," "allow" for "approve," "let" for "hinder," "prevent" for "precede," "conversation" for "conduct," and so forth. Such words are grossly misleading today.

Much of the grammar of the King James Version is not in current usage. "Which" was characteristically employed for "who"; thus in Philippians 4:13 the King James reads, "I can do all things through Christ which strengtheneth me." Likewise "his" was used for "its"; so the King James reads, "salt has lost his savour" (Matt. 5:13). "Cherubims" is found in Hebrews 9:5 instead of the correct plural form, "cherubim."

3. The King James Version includes errors of translation. In the seventeenth century Greek and Hebrew had only recently become subjects of serious study in many universities of Western Europe. At times, therefore, the translators were confronted

with puzzling problems. Many of these problems were solved with skill, but others were not solved at all. For example, Mark 6:20 of the King James says that Herod put John the Baptist in prison and "observed him," but what is meant is that he "kept him safe." "Abstain from all appearance of evil" is the way the King James treats 1 Thessalonians 5:22. A more correct rendering would be, "Abstain from every form of evil."

The King James translation also inaccurately represented the text by creating distinctions in English that are not found in the Greek. Who would know that "Areopagus" and "Mars' Hill" (Acts 17:19, 22) are different renderings of the same Greek word? The King James in Matthew 25:46 reads, "These shall go away into everlasting punishment, but the righteous into life eternal," as though in the Greek text a distinction is made between "everlasting" and "eternal." The King James refers to "Jeremiah" (Matt. 27:9), "Jeremias" (Matt. 16:14), and "Jeremy" (Matt 2:14), so it is possible for one to suppose that there were several Old Testament prophets with similar names instead of one "Jeremiah." On other occasions the King James fails to preserve the distinctions present in the Greek text. One of the best examples of this is the persistent rendering of "hell" for both "Hades" and "Gehenna." In this way "death" and "hell" are made to be thrown into "the lake of fire" (Rev. 20:14), but a more correct translation would substitute "Hades" for "hell."

The English and American Revisions

These and other shortcomings became subjects of sharp criticism in the nineteenth century, and accordingly in February of 1870 a motion to consider a revision of the King James was passed by the Convocation of the Province of Canterbury. By May of that year proposals for the new revision had been agreed upon, and two separate committees (for Old and New Testaments) were being formed. Each committee was originally composed of twenty-seven scholars, but from time to time the exact number on the committees varied due to deaths, resignations, and new appointments. These committees were joined a little later by two American committees who reviewed the work in progress and communicated their detailed suggestions to the English revisers.

The members of the committees were chosen from various denominations and possessed unimpeachable credentials of scholarship. On the English side were such giants of Biblical studies as B. F. Westcott, F. J. A. Hort, J. B. Lightfoot, R. C. Trench, and A. B. Davidson. The American companies also included great names, such as Philip Schaff, J. H. Thayer, and William Henry Green.

The English companies began their work in June of 1870. The New Testament committee met on 407 days over a period of eleven years, the Old Testament committee on 792 days over a space of fifteen years. On 17 May 1881 the first installment of the long-awaited revision reached its conclusion with the issuance of the New Testament. Four years later, on 19 May 1885, the entire Bible was completed with publication of the Old Testament. The whole work is known in America as the English Revised Version.

This was essentially an English revision. American scholars had indeed cooperated in the undertaking, but in the long run the decisions of the British committees prevailed. Divided opinions hinged mainly on differences between British and American idiom and on distinctions of spelling, with the Americans in general favoring more variations from the time-honored King James. These differences were eventually solved by compromise, with the British agreeing to print the American preferences in an attached appendix, and with the Americans agreeing that they would not issue their proposed edition until fourteen years after publication of the English revision. The result was that the American committees, which continued to meet after the British disbanded, put out their edition of the revision in 1901. This edition is known as the American Standard Version and differs little from the English Revised Version, except on points of idiom, spelling, word order, and the like. Of the two revisions, the American Standard Version is naturally preferred in this country and has enjoyed wide circulation and approval.

What can be said in favor of the American revision? First, the revision of 1901 is based on a Greek text which is far superior to that employed by the King James translators. Many of the earlier and most important New Testament manuscripts that were not known in 1611 were accessible to the revision committee, and accordingly its translation was based on these manuscripts. Of all the advantages of recent revisions and translations, this one is chief: an improved textual base underlying the more recent translations.

Second, the revisers have rendered their text more accurately. This is due partly to an advanced knowledge of the original languages and partly to the unvarying ambition of the committee to produce a translation that was meticulously exact.

Third, the revisers cleared up the misleading archaisms of the King James. A few noted examples of improvements in this respect are "spoke first to him" for "prevented him" (Matt. 17:25); "baggage" for "carriages" (Acts 21:15); "made a circuit" for "fetched a compass" (Acts 28:13); "hinder" for "let" (Rom. 1:13); "in nothing be anxious" for "be careful for nothing" (Phil. 4:6); and "grandchildren" for "nephews" (1 Tim. 5:4).

Nevertheless, the American revision did not escape criticism. Much of its criticism was to be expected, for people naturally resist any unfamiliar alterations made in their familiar Bibles. Other criticisms of the revision were justified. Many archaisms had been removed, but others were retained: "glory" for "praise" (Matt. 6:2), "dispute" for "discuss" (Mark 9:34), "doctor" for "teacher" (Luke 5:17), "allege" for "prove" (Acts 17:3), and so forth. Other archaisms actually were created in order to give to the text a "Biblical" flavor. Terms such as "aforetime," "would fain," "howbeit," "lest haply," "us-ward" and "you-ward" are multiplied in the American Standard Version. The net result was that what the American Standard gained in accuracy and consistency over the King James it lost in naturalness and beauty of English style. It breathed of stuffiness and lacked the plain and direct character of the primitive Biblical writings. The comment of Charles H. Spurgeon on the Revised New Testament was typical of many criticisms—"strong in Greek, weak in English." But in spite of these shortcomings the English and American revisions far excelled the illustrious King James. Now it was possible for the English-speaking world to come closer than ever before to the original Bible messages.

The Revised Standard Version

The beginning of the Revised Standard Version goes back to the year 1929. With the expiration of the copyright of the American Standard Version, a new committee of scholars was appointed. In due course it was decided that a new revision should be made that embodied the best results of modern scholarship and yet preserved the literary qualities of the King James translation.

By this time, however, the country had been plunged into the depths of a depression, and funds could not be raised to make the proposed revision a reality. It was not until 1936 that the necessary funds were secured, and shortly afterward the newly constituted committee began its work. By the summer of 1943 the nine members of the New Testament group, which included such well-known scholars as Edgar Goodspeed and James Moffatt, had completed their work. They had met together over the years on 145 days, much additional work having been done by means of correspondence and smaller meetings of the committee. Yet because of wartime restrictions the first edition of the New Testament did not appear until 11 February 1946. Meanwhile, the Old Testament committee continued its labors that finally climaxed with the publication of the complete Bible on 30 September 1952.

There are in general three reasons for the appearance of the Revised Standard Version: (1) a recognition of the many inadequacies of the King James, (2) the failure of the English and American revisions to overcome all of these inadequacies, and (3) the discovery of new resources of knowledge which would warrant, even if the recent versions had been fully adequate, a new revision that included the results of these discoveries.

Coming a half century later, the Revised Standard Version was able to take into account fully the labors of Westcott and Hort (see chapter 10) and other text-critical advances due mainly to the recovery of many Biblical papyri. Besides, the new revision committee, with a vast store of secular papyri at hand, at times could be more precise in its renderings. Some examples of this precision are: "after the sabbath" for "late on the sabbath" (Matt. 28:1); "until an opportune time" for "for a season" (Luke 4:13); "only" for "only begotten" (John 1:14, 18; 3:16, 18; 1 John 4:9); "all of them" for "both of them" (Acts 19:16); "God's field" for "God's husbandry" (1 Cor. 3:9); "peddlers of God's word" for "corrupting the word of God" (2 Cor. 2:17); and "in idleness" for "disorderly" (2 Thess. 3:6). These and many other examples demonstrate the high quality of translation represented in the Revised Standard Version.

Perhaps the greatest gain of the Revised Standard Version over its predecessors is its readability. The Bible, of all books, should be in language that is understandable and easy to read. The Revised Standard Version seeks to recapture the beauty of the King James style in a way that is clear and pleasing to the reader. The American Standard Version in Matthew 21:41 crudely reads, "he will miserably destroy those miserable men"; but the Revised Standard reads, "he will put those wretches to a miserable death." The cumbersome rendering "wherefore neither thought I myself worthy to come unto thee" (Luke 7:7) becomes simply "therefore I did not presume to come to you."

But the Revised Standard Version also has its faults. To give a few examples, it would be better to render "desert" for "wilderness" (Matt. 3:3); "sea monster" for "whale" (Matt. 12:40); "convict" for "convince" (John 16:8); "decided" for "determined" (Acts 11:29); "and then fell away" for "if they then commit apostasy" (Heb. 6:6); and "guaranteed" for "interposed" (Heb. 6:17).

The New Revised Standard Version

After the publication of the Revised Standard Version in 1952, the revision committee continued to meet periodically and over the years made minor changes in the translation. In 1974 a newly constituted committee began work on a revision of the Revised Standard Version. When the question arose concerning the name of the new revision, fortunately one name in particular was not chosen—the Improved Revised Standard, the IRS version![1]

Under the leadership of Professor Bruce M. Metzger, a committee of around thirty members worked at scheduled times for about fifteen years. Their assigned task was to improve the Revised Standard Version by (1) altering some of its paragraph structure and punctuation, (2) reducing archaisms that had not been entirely removed, (3) striving for greater accuracy and clarity, and (4) eliminating all masculine-oriented language when references are made to both men and women.[2]

The New Revised Standard Version was published in 1990. It is not a new translation. It is a revision of the Revised Standard Version of 1946–52, in the line of the American Standard and King James Versions that goes back to Tyndale. This means, on the one hand, that the New Revised Standard Version is privileged to share in an honored tradition and, on the other hand, that its choice of language is restricted to this tradition. Also, because of this tradition, the New Revised Standard necessarily must seek to be as literal as possible yet free when a word-for-word rendering fails to convey clearly the meaning of the text.

Readers of this new version will notice two things in particular. First, "thee" and "thou," and similar outdated forms, are not used in language addressed to God. Matthew 6:9 reads, "Our Father in heaven,/ hallowed be your name." Second, in cases where the original languages refer to men and women in general, male-oriented language is not used. Instead of "man shall not live by bread alone" (Matt. 4:4 RSV) the New Revised Standard Version reads, "One does not live by bread alone."

As we come to evaluate the New Revised Standard Version, clearly much can be said in its favor. The New Revised Standard Version had the distinct advantage of having an illustrious predecessor, the Revised Standard Version. And it must be said to its credit that the New Revised Standard Version has preserved those qualities that have made the Revised Standard Version such an excellent translation.

But are there any real gains in the new version? Was it really necessary to revise the Revised Standard Version?

In order to answer the above questions, let us choose at random the short letter of 1 Timothy to compare the newer version with the older one. Without wishing to notice every detail, here is a checklist of improvements in the New Revised Standard Version: "instruct" for "charge" (1:3); "innocent" for "just" (1:9); "slave traders" for "kidnappers" (1:10); "decently in suitable clothing" for "sensible in seemly apparel" (2:9); "old wives tales" for "silly myths" (4:7); "exhorting" for "preaching" (4:13); "put on the list" for "enrolled" (5:9); "their sinful desires alienate them from Christ" for "they grow wanton against Christ" (5:11); "manage their households" for "rule their households" (5:14); "ordain" for "laying on of hands" (5:22); and "trapped" for "fall into a snare" (6:9).

On the other hand, concerning bishops and deacons, the New Revised Standard Version states that they are to be "married only once" (3:2, 12; cf. 5:9). But since this is only one of several possible meanings, it would be better to have "the husband of one wife."[3] Elsewhere, in 1 Timothy 4:14, instead of "the council of the elders," why not simply "the elders"?

Certainly the most difficult problem the committee faced was how to deal with masculine terms that often have a generic sense. For example, how should the word "brothers" be rendered? In the New Testament the word refers not just to physical brothers but also to human beings (Heb. 2:11, 17) and to Christian believers (Acts 9:30; Rom. 1:13; 1 Tim. 6:2). These distinctions are clearly set forth in the New Revised Standard Version. Many of us may differ on how these and similar passages should be translated, but we should recognize that it is extremely difficult to choose language that is both stylistically and Biblically correct.

Other Translations

Thus far we have focused attention on translations that are in the Tyndale–King James tradition. But many other English translations have been made that are entirely independent of this tradition.[4] Several of these demand special consideration.

1. The New English Bible. The publication of the New English Bible New Testament coincided with the 350th anniversary of the King James Version, but its historic importance lies in the fact that it is a complete departure from the respected ancestry of the Tyndale–King James tradition. Other private translations, of course, did this, but not a translation produced by a group of representative Protestant scholars.

The New English Bible embodies a new principle of translation. The older revisions, especially the Revised Version of 1881–85, were scrupulously literal. Translators insisted that a version was "faithful" only if it met the word-for-word requirement. But the New English Bible, following the precedent set by private translations, broke away from the word-for-word principle by replacing Greek constructions and idioms with those of contemporary English. The New English Bible, then, is a sense-for-sense translation rather than a word-for-word translation.

Any translation that abandons the word-for-word principle leaves itself open to criticism, and the New English Bible has proved to be no exception. The point of concern, however, should be how *accurate* the New English Bible is in conveying the Biblical message. John 1:1 may be taken as an illustration. The New English Bible reads, "When all things began, the Word already was. The Word dwelt with God, and what God was, the Word was." Here is a very beautiful and accurate translation, but it is not one that is word-for-word.

As one would expect, the language of the New English Bible is different. The translators have tried to use the vocabulary of contemporary speech. In this respect it has largely measured up to its intentions. But for the American reader at times its choice of words leaves much to be desired. Reading through the New Testament, one is able to accumulate quite a list of non-American terms and expressions. Fortunately, the Revised English Bible has cleared up many of these problems, as will be discussed a little later in this chapter.

The New English Bible Old Testament, along with a revised edition of the New Testament, appeared in 1970. From the outset the publication of the Old Testament was greeted with reserve and caution. Here, to be sure, was a translation that could be rather easily understood, but here also was a translation that departed considerably from the standard Hebrew text. For example, the Book of Zechariah rearranges arbitrarily the sequence of the text. Zechariah 3:1–10 is transposed to follow 4:14; 4:4–10 is made to follow 3:10; 13:7–9 is placed at the end of chapter 11; and so forth. In the Book of Job, for instance, twenty-three passages are transposed from their regular order to other places in the text. In addition, one often finds at the bottom of the page the note "probable reading." Here the reader needs to be on guard, for the "probable reading" frequently is highly conjectural and not necessarily "probable" at all.

2. The New American Standard Bible. This is a revision and not a completely new translation. Sponsored by the Lockman Foundation of the State of California, the New American Standard was first published in 1963. The New Testament was issued at this time, followed by the Old Testament in 1971. The New American Standard Bible was produced because it was felt that the American Standard Version of 1901 was disappearing too rapidly from the modern scene. Thus the aim of the Lockman Foundation was to preserve in contemporary form the American Standard Version, which in the view of the appointed translators embodied the ideal of what a translation ought to be.

The natural question to ask is whether the Lockman Foundation has attained its desired goal. Has the New American Standard translation truly preserved the *old* American Standard?

It is a mistake to think of the New American Standard Bible as a modernized American Standard Version. The new translation has indeed eliminated most of the out-of-date language found in the American revision of 1901, and it has made other improvements as well. Yet in other respects the new translation is not necessarily better. One noticeable feature of the New American Standard is the printing of each verse as a separate unit, resorting to the practice of the King James Version instead of that of the American Standard which appears in paragraph form. Another feature of the New American Standard is its use of precise distinctions in the tenses of verbs. This may be thought commendable, but often minute distinctions are made which cannot be correctly and consistently applied. This, of course, was not attempted by the American Standard Version of 1901.

Although the New American Standard offers a number of advantages over the 1901 American Standard, many of its improvements were already present in the Revised Standard Version of 1946–52.[5] In 1995 a new edition of the New American Standard Version was issued.

3. The New International Version. Of the more recent translations, none has been accepted more widely than the New International Version. Although not published until 1973 (New Testament) and 1978 (Old Testament), its beginning traces back to the 1950s, in particular to dissatisfaction at that time with the Revised Standard Version. Evangelicals and others were unhappy with a number of passages in the newly introduced Revised Standard because, in their view, these passages reflected a liberal theological bias on the part of the translators. After some time a committee of international scholars was formed to produce an entirely new translation that hopefully would surpass in accuracy and readability all previous translations. The ultimate product of these scholars is the New International Version.

What is to be said in favor of this translation? How good is the New International Version, and how does it compare with other translations?

Undoubtedly, the New International Version, in both Old and New Testaments, in clarity and readability, offers considerable gains. Because it is not tied to a literal word-for-word translation theory, otherwise obscure expressions frequently are turned into phrases with meaning and appeal. A brief list of such improvements may be made, for example, from the opening chapters of Acts: "place of leadership" for "office" (1:20); "converts to Judaism" for "proselytes" (2:10); "all people" for "all flesh" (2:17); "corrupt" for "crooked" (2:40); "Solomon's Colonnade" for "Solomon's portico" (3:11); "from the Lord" for "from the presence of the Lord" (3:19); "miraculous signs" for "signs" (5:12); "murderous threats" for "threats and murder" (9:1); "prayed regularly" for "prayed constantly" (10:1). This list, of course, could be lengthened throughout the rest of Acts and other books of the New Testament.

Improvements to the readability of the New International Version may, however, be counterbalanced with a list of terms not as easily understood by those with a limited vocabulary. Turning again to the Book of Acts, the following examples stand out: "bewilderment" (2:6), "conspire" (4:27), "dispersed" (5:36), "shrieks" (8:7), "baffled" (9:22), "clutches" (12:11), "abusively" (13:45), "appease" (16:39), "defying" (17:7), "sneered" (17:32), "misdemeanor" (18:14), "obstinate" (19:9), "publicly maligned" (19:9), "venture" (19:31), "dissuaded" (21:14), "pretext" (23:15), "desecrate" (24:6), and "obsession" (26:11). This sample list likewise could be extended through the remainder of the New Testament. One wonders if the use of such terms is either necessary or helpful.

All in all, the translators of the New International Version have produced a work that is useful for many readers. On the other hand, the New International Version is by no means the standard *par excellence* of all recent translations. As to accuracy, the New International Version does quite well. As to style, the New International Version is often abrupt and uneven in quality.[6] Recent editions of the New International Version use gender-inclusive language.

4. The Revised English Bible. Making its appearance in 1989, the Revised English Bible claims to be a "substantial revision" of the New English Bible. In 1961, when the New English New Testament was first published, it included a number of words and phrases that clearly were not contemporary in the United States. Most of these non-American expressions are no longer present in the Revised English Bible, but others still remain. For example, in the Gospel of Mark the following occur: "cornfields" and "ears of corn" (2:23), "went to synagogue" (3:1), "took to their

heels" (5:14), "at the instance of his brother" (6:17), "said an oath" (6:23), "goes rigid" (9:18), "tethered" (11:2), "fetch" (12:15), "taken aback" (12:17), and "who had committed murder in the rising" (15:7). These expressions may be understandable, but they are not generally used in America.

5. Other translations. Besides the translations already discussed, several others should be noticed. The New King James Bible has an appeal for many of those who have long used the King James Version. Since 1611 there have been many changes in the English language, and an updated version is a great boon to many readers. Contrary to its claims, however, the New King James is not the first major revision of the old King James. The Revised Version of 1881–85, effected by careful British scholarship, was a thorough overhaul of the King James Version, followed by the American Standard, Revised Standard, and New Revised Standard Versions. This raises the serious question whether there is a need for the New King James Bible at all.

The Good News Bible (1976) has been a pioneer of translations that employ a simple vocabulary and short sentence structure. This type of translation is particularly helpful for those who have difficulty in reading, although a translation of this kind has obvious limitations. Other works such as The Living Bible (1971) and The Message (New Testament, 1993) are paraphrases and not translations in the true sense. A paraphrase is not in itself bad, but these often go far beyond the limits of the Biblical text.

Other translations could be mentioned and others are sure to come in the future. Each translation has and will have pluses and minuses. In evaluating translations, the best procedure is to read a passage or chapter or book as a whole, and then decide about certain details by comparing translation with translation.

Summary

No one translation is infallible. With the advance of time, it was inevitable that revisions would have to be made of the classic King James Version. The English Revised and American

Standard Versions have largely met the needs of revision, especially in providing translations that are based on earlier and more reliable manuscripts. But changes of time and a number of manuscript discoveries have made more recent revisions and translations desirable.

From the beginning of the twentieth century on, there has been a surge of new translations. All of them have their faults, but some of them are especially good and can be of great help to the Bible reader. Among these are the Revised Standard Version, the New International Version, and the New Revised Standard Version. Other recent translations, too, are of much value to varying degrees. The Scripture references cited in this chapter should be studied carefully and compared with the other translations. In this way the individual Bible student can decide which translation is most useful for him or her, and at the same time see the value of all the translations.

For Discussion

1. What are some of the basic weaknesses of the King James Version that called for a new revision?
2. Relate something of the background of the English Revised Version. What brought about the American Standard Version? How would you distinguish between these translations?
3. What are some of the chief merits of the American Standard Version? What are some of its shortcomings?
4. What are the strengths and weaknesses of the following: (1) Revised Standard Version, (2) New Revised Standard Version, (3) New International Version? How are they similar and yet different?
5. You might want to make an independent study and evaluation of other recent translations. In your opinion, what are their strengths and weaknesses?

18

"My Words Will Not Pass Away"

racing the Bible down through the centuries presents the human side of how we got the Bible. From a different standpoint, the story of how we got the Bible begins and ends with God. God is Light, the Source of Light, both physical and spiritual. Ultimately, then, the question of how we got the Bible leads us to the throne of God.

In Mark 13:31 Jesus said, "Heaven and earth will pass away, but my words will not pass away." Here Jesus makes two claims. First, he claims that his words are divine: the world will pass away but his words will not. Therefore, his words are not from the world. Second, because his words are divine, Jesus claims that his words will stand forever.

"My Words"

The claim made by Jesus for his words, that they are divine, is the claim that the Bible as a whole makes for itself. The Apostle Paul wrote, "All Scripture is inspired by God and is useful for teaching, for reproof, for correction, and for training in righteousness, so that everyone who belongs to God may be proficient, equipped for every good work" (2 Tim. 3:16–17 NRSV). The term "Scripture" is here used in a special sense,

(201)

referring to the canonical writings of the Old Testament. It was Paul's belief that the Old Testament writings had come from God, that they were literally *God-breathed.*

In a similar passage another apostle said, "And we have the prophetic word made more sure. You will do well to pay attention to this as to a lamp shining in a dark place, until the day dawns and the morning star rises in your hearts. First of all you must understand this, that no prophecy of scripture is a matter of one's own interpretation, because no prophecy ever came by the impulse of man, but men moved by the Holy Spirit spoke from God" (2 Peter 1:19–21). The Old Testament writers, Peter said, did not invent or devise the messages of their books. What each of them said and wrote was due to an influence outside themselves: they spoke from God as the Holy Spirit guided them. Each of these passages plainly affirms that the Old Testament is of divine origin.

If the Old Testament prophets were inspired by God, is it conceivable that New Testament men, including the Savior and his apostles, would possess less inspiration than they? We expect to find, therefore, an inspiration in the New Testament at least equal to that of the Old. And this is what we do find. The Lord often contrasted his teachings with Moses' law (Matt. 5:27–48), leaving the unavoidable impression that a person greater than Moses had come. His chosen apostles were endowed with such authority that whatever they required on earth became a requirement in heaven (Matt. 16:19; cf. 18:18; John 20:23). The church at Corinth was expected to acknowledge that what the Apostle Paul wrote to them was "a command of the Lord" (1 Cor. 14:37). And the early New Testament churches did acknowledge such apostolic authority. They received the words of the apostles "not as the word of men but as what it really is, the word of God" (1 Thess. 2:13).

It may be objected that this is circular reasoning, that inspiration is assumed in order to prove inspiration. But this is not true. It is assumed, however, that the men who wrote the Bible were honest men and were of a sound mind. If they were sane and sober-minded, they would not be susceptible to fanciful visions and hallucinations; if they were honest, they would not intentionally deceive.

Much of the uniqueness of the Bible rests on its unique claims. Permitting it to speak for itself, the Bible claims to be from God. This claim comes from honest, straight-thinking men and deserves consideration. The claim does not authenticate the truthfulness of the claim, but the contents of the Bible, with its theme of salvation and its strong moral fiber, support it. Jesus' ethical principles, for example, are either human or divine. The Bible says that they are divine. The *claims* of the Bible plus the *contents* of the Bible equal a *convincing case* for the Bible as the inspired Word of God.

"Will Not Pass Away"

Jesus promised that his words would not pass away. Divine Providence through the centuries has been working in many ways to fulfill this promise. Viewing the situation in the twenty-first century, many evidences can be observed which show that the Lord is preserving his Word.

1. The quantity of materials available on the Bible text. The number of textual documents, including manuscripts and versions, is so vast that it practically defies calculation. A conservative guess would be at least 20,000. Of these, as we have seen, some 5,300 alone are manuscripts of the New Testament. It is interesting to compare this figure with the manuscripts by which the principal Greek and Roman writings have come down to us. The history of Thucydides, for example, which was written about 400 B.C., is available today on the basis of eight manuscripts, while the few books that remain of the Roman historian Tacitus (c. A.D. 100) have survived on the margin of two manuscripts. In other words many of the great classical writings are transmitted to the present day by no more than a handful of manuscripts. This being true, and since no one really questions the textual foundations of the classics, why should a mist of doubt prevail over the Bible text? If any book

from ancient times has descended to us without substantial loss or alteration, it is the Bible.

The Bible is the best-attested book from the ancient world! This has prompted Sir Frederic Kenyon to say, "The number of manuscripts of the New Testament, of early translations from it, and of quotations from it in the oldest writers of the Church, is so large that it is practically certain that the true reading of every doubtful passage is preserved in some one or other of these ancient authorities. This can be said of no other ancient book in the world."[1]

2. The quality of materials available on the Bible text. Information on the Bible text is not only abundant but reliable. The celebrated Vatican and Sinaitic Manuscripts are only about two centuries removed from the close of the apostolic age, and even this period is partially filled in by recently discovered papyrus documents. If there were no papyri, the text of the New Testament would still stand in a remarkably advantageous position.

This can be seen by further reference to the classics mentioned above. The two manuscripts of Tacitus' works are of late date, one from the ninth century and the other from the eleventh, and none of the manuscripts of Thucydides, except for fragments, date any earlier. Copies of Thucydides are thus about 1,300 years later than the date of their original composition, yet no effort is made to discount these copies in spite of such a wide interval of time. These examples cited from the classics are not isolated cases, for the fact is that the vast majority of writings from ancient times have been preserved on late-date manuscripts. By contrast, our New Testament text rests on manuscripts that are very near to the date of their original composition. The text of the New Testament, as compared with other ancient books, holds a unique and enviable rank.

Summary

Perhaps it is wise now to summarize the main points in each of the preceding chapters in order that the essential features of the Bible's history may be more firmly fixed in our minds.

1. For the history of the Bible the most important writing materials are leather, papyrus, and parchment or vellum. Leather was principally used in the Old Testament period, while the New Testament books were undoubtedly first penned on papyrus. About the fourth century A.D. papyrus was replaced by parchment, with the result that practically all the New Testament manuscripts today are inscribed on vellum or parchment.

2. Our Bible is an amazing collection of books. The various books of the Bible often have been differently but logically arranged. The Bible was originally written in three languages: Hebrew, Aramaic, and Greek. The New Testament was written in Greek, the Old Testament was written in Hebrew, with some sections in Aramaic.

3. Manuscripts of the New Testament are of two classes: uncials and cursives or minuscules. Minuscules are those written in small letters, while uncials are those found in large, capital letters. Of the two, the uncials are earlier and are the more important as authorities on the New Testament text. The three famous uncials are the Vatican, the Sinaitic, and the Alexandrian Manuscripts.

4. Among the famous uncials the Sinaitic Manuscript deserves special attention. Found by Constantin Tischendorf, it remains of great interest because of its exciting discovery and publication, its being made a gift to the Czar amidst controversy, its subsequent relocation in England, and its new story of the discovery of some of its missing leaves.

5. Two other important uncial manuscripts are Codex Ephraem and Codex Bezae. Other uncial and minuscule manuscripts are likewise valuable. Generally speaking, New Testament manuscripts may be divided into three types of text: Alexandrian, Western, and Byzantine. Of these the Alexandrian is regarded as the best form of the text.

6. Ancient versions of the New Testament add welcomed information on the text. Three versions are very early and are especially noteworthy: the Syriac, the Latin, and the Coptic (Egyptian). It was Jerome who gave us the Latin Vulgate, which

became the standard Bible in Western Europe, and from it the earliest English translations were made.

7. Among the many Latin manuscripts that have survived, three stand out above all others. Codex Amiatinus is a huge Latin Bible that has an excellent text of the Vulgate. The Lindisfarne Gospels and the Book of Kells are wondrous manuscripts that are often described as the most beautiful books in the world.

8. It was inevitable that transcription mistakes would appear in the production of copies. The task of textual criticism is to detect these mistakes and mark them off from the pure text. With a wealth of information at hand and following rather exact principles, the textual critic is able to do this with a high degree of precision.

9. Textual variants are of different types and degrees of importance. Most variants are obvious slips made by the scribe and present no problem. Others are of no consequence to our present text because they are not found in the most reliable manuscripts. Some represent substantial variation, but in this number no unique Biblical teaching or divine command is involved.

10. Our present New Testament text is a restored or reconstructed Greek text. Westcott and Hort, drawing on the work of their predecessors, are largely responsible for this reconstruction. Our modern Greek text, in contrast to the so-called "Received Text," is based on the earliest and best witnesses.

11. The sands of Egypt have revealed a number of Biblical papyri, some of which predate the Vatican and Sinaitic Manuscripts by 150 years. Because of their early dates, these papyri are extremely valuable and contribute significantly to the solid foundation on which our modern text is based.

12. The work of the Massoretes and other early Jewish scribes has resulted in a carefully copied edition of the Old Testament text. The recently discovered Dead Sea Scrolls, especially the two Isaiah scrolls, give unquestioned support to the reliability of our accepted Old Testament text.

13. Ancient versions of the Old Testament play an important role as witnesses to the text. The Septuagint, the Aramaic

Targums, the Samaritan Pentateuch, the Syriac, and Jerome's Latin Vulgate remain of great value.

14. The term *canon* applies to those books that are included in the Bible as authoritative Scripture. Separate books became a part of the canon gradually. Much clear-cut and indisputable evidence exists as to which books were and were not counted as Scripture.

15. The "Apocrypha" usually refers to a group of about fifteen books not included in our Old Testament. The Apocrypha represents different types of literature: (1) historical, (2) legendary, (3) prophetic, and (4) ethical/devotional. Many sound reasons can be given for not including these books in our Bibles, the chief reason being that they have never been accepted in the Hebrew canon of the Old Testament.

16. William Tyndale is the true father of the English Bible. He was the first to translate the New Testament in English based on a Greek text. He himself suffered martyrdom, but his ambition to put the Bible in the hands of the people lived on, eventually resulting in the appearance of the illustrious King James Version.

17. Increasing knowledge of the Bible text and related matters made it necessary to revise the King James translation. The main revisions are the American Standard, the Revised Standard, and the New Revised Standard Versions. Each of these translations has its faults, but each also has its great advantages. Other translations have made their appearance, including the well-accepted New International Version. Besides their readability, the most important advantage of recent translations is that they are based on early manuscripts and thus stand closer to the original inspired message.

Conclusion

We now bring to a close our study of how we got the Bible. It is a remarkable story, far reaching in scope, extending to both Old and New Testaments, to the manuscripts that lie behind them, and to the translations that have been made from them.

Ours is the privilege to study this remarkable story. It is the history of the most important book in the world. For those who have passed it on from generation to generation, for the legacy of their undying devotion, we owe an incalculable debt. "Every word that proceeds from the mouth of God" is important (cf. Matt. 4:4). This is why we study about it, and why this book is written.

In the end, it is comforting and reassuring to know that Jesus' words will not pass away. This promise has been tested by centuries and has not failed. "The grass withers, and the flower falls, but the word of the Lord abides forever" (1 Peter 1:24–25).

The Word of God is accessible to English-speaking people in many translations. Some translations are good, others are better. None of the major translations are so bad and no Greek text is so faulty as to lead one away from "the lamb of God who takes away the sin of the world." To be sure, improvements of translation ought to be welcomed and appreciated. But the important thing is that the individual use the translation he or she favors.

Because the modern farmer has a variety of new equipment, this does not guarantee a successful crop. The equipment must be used. Likewise, in a period where God's grace abounds in the supply of new and better helps for Bible study, let us not presume that the presence of the equipment can substitute for the use of it. May God grant that we shall continue to be a people of one book, and that book the Bible.

For Discussion

1. What two important passages claim that the Old Testament is inspired? What evidence is there to show that the apostles in New Testament times also possessed inspiration?

2. Is inspiration assumed in order to prove inspiration? If not, what is assumed?
3. How does the quantity of evidence on the New Testament text compare with the quantity available for other ancient books?
4. Why is it accurate to say the Bible is the best-attested book from the ancient world? How does this affect your faith in God and in the authority of the Bible?
5. Summarize some of the main points in a study of how we got the Bible. What are some of the points that have been especially helpful to you?

Notes

Chapter 1: The Making of Ancient Books

1. D. J. Wiseman, "Archaeology and Scripture," *Westminster Theological Journal* 33 (1971): 138–39.

2. For an interesting account of the discovery of the tunnel, see James B. Pritchard, *Archaeology and the Old Testament* (Princeton, N.J.: Princeton University Press, 1958), 36–42. On the inscription itself, see V. Sasson, "The Siloam Tunnel Inscription," *Palestine Exploration Quarterly* 14 (1982): 111–17; Simon B. Parker, "Siloam Inscription Memorializes Engineering Achievement," *Biblical Archaeological Review* 20 (July/August 1994): 36–38.

3. On the Moabite Stone and its discovery, see Siegfried H. Horn, "Why the Moabite Stone Was Blown to Pieces," *Biblical Archaeology Review* 12 (May/June 1986): 50–61.

4. See J. Hoftijzer, "The Prophet Balaam in a 6th Century Aramaic Inscription," *Biblical Archaeologist* 39 (1976): 11–17. For an excellent discussion, see P. Kyle McCarter Jr., *Ancient Inscriptions: Voices from the Biblical World* (Washington, D.C.: Biblical Archaeology Society, 1996), 96–98; on ink-on-plaster writing, 64, 105–6.

5. For an interesting account on the use of clay tablets, see Edward Chiera, *They Wrote on Clay*, ed. G. G. Cameron (Chicago: University of Chicago Press, 1938). Also, see C. B. F. Walker, *Cuneiform*, no. 3, *Reading the Past* (London: British Museum, 1987).

6. See Robert Biggs, "The Ebla Tablets: An Interim Perspective," *Biblical Archaeologist* 43 (1980): 76–87; Paolo Matthiae, *Ebla, An Empire Rediscovered* (Garden City, NY: Doubleday, 1981); Giovanni Pettinato, *The Archives of Ebla* (Garden City, NY: Doubleday, 1981). The number of tablets is difficult to estimate, since thousands are fragmentary. See Biggs's article, "Ebla Texts," in D. N. Freedman et al., eds., *The Anchor Bible Dictionary*, vol. 2 (New York: Doubleday, 1992), 263–70.

7. As quoted by David Diringer, *The Hand-Produced Book* (New York: Philosophical Library, 1953); reprint, *The Book before Printing: Ancient, Medieval and Oriental* (New York: Dover, 1982), 109.

8. See Gabriel Barkay, "The Divine Name Found in Jerusalem," *Biblical Archaeology Review* 9 (March/April 1983): 14–19; Michael D. Coogan, "10 Great Finds," *Biblical Archaeology Review* 21 (May/June, 1985): 45.

9. See A. Demsky and M. Kochavi, "An Alphabet from the Days of the Judges," *Biblical Archaeology Review* 4 (September/October, 1978): 23–25.

10. For a good discussion of the Lachish letters, see Pritchard, *Archaeology and the Old Testament*, 10–18. On the Samaria ostraca, see Ivan T. Kaufman, "The Samaria Ostraca: An Early Witness to Hebrew Writing," *Biblical Archaeologist* 45 (1982): 229–239.

11. On the many uses of papyrus, see Napthali Lewis, *Papyrus in Classical Antiquity* (Oxford: Clarendon, 1974), 21–32.

12. Pliny, *Natural History* 13.23.74.

13. A few, however, were written on papyrus, a practice which may go back much earlier. See Emanuel Tov, *Textual Criticism of the Hebrew Bible* (Minneapolis: Fortress, 1992), 202.

Chapter 2: The Birth of the Bible

1. Eric G. Turner, *The Typology of the Early Codex* (Philadelphia: University of Pennsylvania Press, 1977), 1.

2. C. H. Roberts, "The Codex," *Proceedings of the British Academy* 40 (1954): 169–204; C. H. Roberts and T. C. Skeat, *The Birth of the Codex* (London: Oxford University Press, 1983). For a good summary, see T. C. Skeat, "Early Christian Book Production: Papyri and Manuscripts," in P. R. Ackroyd, C. F. Evans, G. W. H. Lampe, and S. L. Greenslade, eds., *Cambridge History of the Bible*, vol. 2 (Cambridge: Cambridge University Press, 1963–1970), 68–72.

3. See Roberts' impressive manuscript statistics in *The Birth of the Codex*, 38–44. T. C. Skeat has suggested that Christians adopted the codex because only a codex could contain all four Gospels. Skeat, "The Oldest Manuscript of the Gospels," *New Testament Studies* 43 (1997): 31.

4. The dating of Moses depends on the dating of the Exodus, which is still much debated. Generally, two dates are advocated: an earlier date, c. 1450 B.C., and a later date, c. 1250 B.C.

5. Josephus, *Against Apion* 1. 8. Actually, Josephus marks off the interval of the Old Testament books as being from Moses to the time of the Persian King Artaxerxes. The time of Artaxerxes (465–425 B.C.) was the time of Ezra, Nehemiah, and Malachi.

6. On the precise nature of New Testament Greek, Nigel Turner has taken the lead in arguing that it is actually a dialect of "Jewish Greek." See especially his *Christian Words* (Nashville: Thomas Nelson, 1982). Opposite Turner, see G. H. R. Horsely, "The Fiction of 'Jewish Greek,'" in *New Documents Illustrating Early Christianity*, vol. 5, *Linguistic Essays* (Sydney: Macquarie University Press, 1989), 5–40.

7. Bruce M. Metzger, "When Did Scribes Begin to Use Writing Desks?" in *Historical and Literary Studies: Pagan, Jewish, and Christian* (Leiden: E. J. Brill, 1968), 123–37; G. M. Parassoglou, "A Roll upon His Knees," *Yale Classical Studies* 28 (1985): 273–75. On equipment used by the scribe, see Metzger, *Manuscripts of the Greek Bible: An Introduction to Greek Paleography* (New York: Oxford University Press, 1985), 17–18.

8. On early Christian libraries, see Harry Y. Gamble, *Books and Readers in the Early Church: A History of Early Christian Texts* (New Haven: Yale University Press, 1995), 144–76, 196–202; on early scriptoria, 120–25.

9. On scribal notes, see Bruce M. Metzger, *The Text of the New Testament: Its Transmission, Corruption, and Restoration*, 3d ed. (New York: Oxford University Press, 1992), 17–21; also Metzger, *Manuscripts of the Greek Bible*, 20, 104.

10. *Biblical Archaeologist* 45 (1982): 143–53.

Chapter 3: Manuscripts of the New Testament

1. On the dating of New Testament manuscripts, see Bruce M. Metzger, *Manuscripts of the Greek Bible* (New York: Oxford University Press, 1981), 49–51.

2. Frederic Kenyon, *Our Bible and the Ancient Manuscripts*, rev. A. W. Adams (New York: Harper & Brothers, 1958), 202–3.

3. Aleph is the first letter of the Hebrew alphabet.

4. See M. Spinka, "Acquisition of the Codex Alexandrinus," *Review of Religion* 16 (1936): 10–29. On the Alexandrian and Sinaitic Manuscripts, see H. I. Bell, *The Codex Sinaiticus and the Codex Alexandrinus*, 2d ed., rev. T. C. Skeat (London: Trustees of the British Museum, 1963).

Chapter 4: The Sinaitic Manuscript

1. C. Tischendorf, *Codex Sinaiticus: The Ancient Biblical Manuscript Now in the British Museum: Tischendorf's Story and Argument Related by Himself*, 8th ed. (London: Lutterworth Press, 1933), 16–17.

2. Ibid., 17.

3. C. Tischendorf, *Travels in the East*, trans. W. E. Shuckard (London: Longman, Brown, Green, and Longman, 1847), 2.

4. Tischendorf, *Tischendorf's Story*, 23–24. This quotation, and the one following, is given in full because few readers today have access to Tischendorf's own account.

5. Ibid., 27–28.

6. L. Schneller, *Search on Sinai: The Story of Tischendorf's Life and the Search for a Lost Manuscript*, trans. Dorothee Schroder (London: Epworth, 1939), 71.

7. For a defense of Tischendorf, see *The Mount Sinai Manuscript of the Bible* (London: British Museum, 1934). For the other side, see Ihor Ševčenko, "New Documents on Constantine Tischendorf and the Codex Sinaiticus," *Scriptorium* 18 (1964): 55–80.

8. Tischendorf, *Tischendorf's Story*, 21.

9. Ibid., 33–34.

10. Some of the details are given by James Bentley, *Secrets of Mount Sinai: The Story of Finding the World's Oldest Bible—Codex Sinaiticus* (Garden City, N.Y.: Doubleday, 1986). Bentley's work, although interestingly written, is uneven in quality.

11. *Scribes and Correctors of the Codex Sinaiticus*, by H. J. M. Milne and T. C. Skeat (London: British Museum, 1938), remains the major work on the Sinaitic Manuscript.

12. J. K. Elliott, *Codex Sinaiticus and the Simonides Affair*, Analecta Vlatadon 33, ed. P. Christou (Thessaloniki: Patriarchal Institute for Patristic Studies, 1982). See also T. C. F. Stunt, "Some Unpublished Letters of S. P. Tregelles relating to the Codex Sinaiticus," including Tregelles' letter concerning Simonides, *Evangelical Quarterly* 48 (1976): 15–26.

13. Charlesworth's articles in the *Biblical Archaeologist* (vols. 41–3, 1978–80) have been published under the title *The New Discoveries in St. Catherine's Monastery: A Preliminary Report*, American Schools of Oriental Research Monograph Series 3, ed.

D. N. Freedman (Winona Lake, IN, 1981). See also Charlesworth's note in *The Anchor Bible Dictionary*, vol. 1, p. 1074, and Bentley, *Secrets of Mount Sinai*, 22, 197–208.

Chapter 5: Other New Testament Manuscripts

1. See Bruce M. Metzger, *Manuscripts of the Greek Bible* (New York: Oxford University Press, 1981), 18–19.

2. Robert W. Lyon has corrected Tischendorf's work, but now further corrections are needed. See David C. Parker, "The Majuscule Manuscripts of the New Testament," in *The Text of the New Testament in Contemporary Research: Essays on the Status Quaestionis*, ed. Bart D. Ehrman and Michael W. Holmes (Grand Rapids: Eerdmans, 1995), 36; cf. Lyon, "A Re-examination of Codex Ephraemi Rescriptus," *New Testament Studies* (1958–59): 260–72.

3. I am grateful to Mr. Arthur Owen, Keeper of Manuscripts, for allowing me to examine Codex Bezae.

4. For a list of manuscripts now known, with their contents and locations, see Kurt Aland and Barbara Aland, *The Text of the New Testament*, trans. Erroll F. Rhodes (Grand Rapids: Eerdmans, 1987), 96–155. The Nestle-Aland Greek text also has a convenient list.

5. See C. C. Tarelli, "Erasmus' Manuscripts of the Gospels," *Journal of Theological Studies* 44 (1943): 155–62.

6. On the lectionaries, see Ernest C. Colwell and Donald W. Riddle, *Prolegomena to the Study of the Lectionary Text of the Gospels* (Chicago: University of Chicago Press, 1933); John Reumann, "A History of Lectionaries: From the Synagogue at Nazareth to Post-Vatican II," *Interpretation* 31 (1977): 116–30; Carroll D. Osburn, "The Greek Lectionaries of the New Testament," in *The Text of the New Testament in Contemporary Research*, ed. Ehrman and Holmes, 61–74.

Chapter 6: Ancient Versions: The New Testament

1. For the sources on the Diatessaron, see Bruce M. Metzger, *The Early Versions of the New Testament: Their Origin, Transmission, and Limitations* (New York: Oxford University Press, 1977), 10–25. On the versions in general, see also Arthur Vööbus, *Early Versions of the New Testament: Manuscript Studies* (Stockholm: Estonian Theological Society in Exile, 1954).

2. For an interesting biography of Mrs. Smith and Mrs. Gibson, see A. Whigham Price, *The Ladies of Castlebrae* (Gloucester, England: Alan Sutton, 1985).

3. As related by Arthur Vööbus, *Early Versions of the New Testament*, 37.

4. See the fascinating biography of Jerome by J. N. D. Kelly, *Jerome: His Life, Writings, and Controversies* (New York: Harper & Row, 1975).

5. Jerome, Letter 22. 30.

6. Jerome, *Preface to the Four Gospels*.

7. See Kelly, *Jerome*, 88–89. For a thorough discussion, see Metzger, *The Early Versions*, 356–62. For the contrary view, see E. F. Sutcliffe, "Jerome," in *The Cambridge History of the Bible*, vol. 2, ed. G. W. H. Lampe (Cambridge: Cambridge University Press, 1969), 84.

8. Jerome, Letter 27. 1.

Notes

Chapter 7: Manuscripts of Special Interest

1. On illuminated manuscripts, see Christopher de Hamel, *A History of Illuminated Manuscripts* (Oxford: Phaidon, 1986) and David Diringer, *The Illuminated Book: Its History and Production* (New York: Philosophical Library, 1958); also Carl Nordenfalk, *Early Medieval Book Illumination* (New York: Rizzoli, 1988) and Jonathan J. G. Alexander, *Medieval Illuminators and Their Methods of Work* (New Haven: Yale University Press, 1992).

2. Early Christian writers had different explanations of the symbols. See Robin M. Jensen, "Of Cherubim & Gospel Symbols," *Biblical Archaeology Review* 21 (July/August 1995): 43, 65.

3. For a very readable account of this manuscript, see Janet Backhouse, *The Lindisfarne Gospels* (Oxford: Phaidon, 1986).

4. The quotation is given by F. Henry, *The Book of Kells* (New York: Alfred A. Knopf, 1974), 165. Henry's book remains the standard, but see also Peter Brown, *The Book of Kells* (London: Thames and Hudson, 1980).

5. See Christopher de Hamel, *A History of Illuminated Manuscripts*, 40.

Chapter 8: The Text of the New Testament

1. Actually, in the first few years after 1611, there were a number of editions and issues of the King James Version, which made many changes but also introduced new errors.

2. For a discussion of the more important textual variations from Matthew to Revelation, see Bruce M. Metzger's indispensable work, *A Textual Commentary on the Greek New Testament*, 2d ed. (London: United Bible Societies, 1994).

3. On the practice of New Testament textual criticism, see Bruce M. Metzger, *The Text of the New Testament: Its Transmission, Corruption, and Restoration*, 3d ed. (New York: Oxford University Press, 1992), 207–46; and Kurt Aland and Barbara Aland, *The Text of the New Testament*, trans. Erroll F. Rhodes (Grand Rapids: Eerdmans, 1987), 275–311.

Chapter 9: Significance of Textual Variations

1. In 1966 Kenneth W. Clark estimated perhaps as many as 300,000 variants. "The Theological Relevance of Textual Variation in Current Criticism of the Greek New Testament," *Journal of Biblical Literature* 85 (1966): 3.

2. The number of variants listed on this page varies slightly, depending on which edition of the Greek text is consulted.

3. The Sinaitic Manuscript reads "Apelles," while Codex Bezae has "Apollonios."

4. B. F. Westcott and F. J. A. Hort, *Introduction [and] Appendix*, vol. 2 of *The New Testament in the Original Greek* (London: Macmillan and Co., 1881), appendix p. 87. On this and other textual variants, see Bruce M. Metzger, *A Textual Commentary on the Greek New Testament*, 2d ed. (London: United Bible Societies, 1994). On this passage, see Gary M. Burge, "A Specific Problem of the New Testament Text and Canon: The Woman Caught in Adultery (John 7:53–8:11)," *Journal of the Evangelical Theological Society* 27 (1984): 141–48.

5. See Metzger, *Textual Commentary*, 102–6, and his *Text of the New Testament*, 226–29. For a defense of Mark 16:9–20, see William F. Farmer, *The Last Twelve Verses*

(215)

of Mark (Cambridge: Cambridge University Press, 1974); cf. J. N. Birdsall's critique of Farmer in *The Journal of Theological Studies* 26 (1975): 151–60.

Chapter 10: Restoring the New Testament Text

1. Bruce M. Metzger, *The Text of the New Testament: Its Transmission, Corruption, and Restoration*, 3d ed. (New York: Oxford University Press, 1992), 86.

2. J. A. Froude, *Life and Letters of Erasmus* (New York: Charles Scribner's Sons, 1912), 127. For more recent works on Erasmus, see Roland H. Bainton, *Erasmus of Christendom* (London: Collins, 1970) and Leon-E. Halkin, *Erasmus: A Critical Biography*, trans. John Tonkin (Oxford: Blackwell, 1993).

3. As given in the invaluable work of S. P. Tregelles, *An Account of the Printed Text of the New Testament: With Remarks on Its Revision upon Critical Principles* (London: Samuel Bagster and Sons, 1854), 35.

4. See Adam Fox, *John Mill and Richard Bentley: A Study of the Textual Criticism of the New Testament 1675–1729* (Oxford: Basil Blackwell, 1954); on Whitby and Collins, see 105–8.

5. Richard Bentley, *Remarks upon a Late Discourse of Free-Thinking, In a Letter to F. H., D. D. by Phileleutherus Lipsiensis*, 8th ed. (Cambridge: J. Bentham, 1743), 88–97. The pamphlet is rare, but most of this important section is reprinted in S. P. Tregelles, *An Account of the Printed Text of the Greek New Testament*, 49–57. For convenience, I have rearranged some of Bentley's statements to form one paragraph.

6. See Graham A. Patrick, *F. J. A. Hort: Eminent Victorian* (Sheffield, England: Almond, 1988). The book, although mainly about Hort, has much to say also about Westcott and their work together. On their Greek text, see especially pp. 76–84.

Chapter 11: Manuscripts from the Sand

1. See Sandra Sider, "Herculaneum's Library in 79 A.D.: The Villa of the Papyri," *Libraries and Culture* 25 (1990): 534–42.

2. Bernard P. Grenfell and Arthur S. Hunt, eds., *The Oxyrhynchus Papyri, Part 1* (London: Egypt Exploration Fund, 1898), 4.

3. T. C. Skeat, "The Oldest Manuscript of the Four Gospels," *New Testament Studies* 43 (1997): 30. See also C. H. Roberts, *Manuscript, Society, and Belief in Early Christian Egypt* (London: Oxford University Press, 1979), 13.

4. Adolf Deissmann, "The New Papyrus Fragment on the Fourth Gospel," *The British Weekly* 99 (12 December 1935): 219.

5. See Eldon Jay Epp, "The Papyrus Manuscripts of the New Testament," in *The Text of the New Testament in Contemporary Research: Essays on the Status Quaestionis*, ed. Bart D. Ehrman and Michael W. Holmes (Grand Rapids: Eerdmans, 1995), 2–13.

6. B. F. Westcott and F. J. A. Hort, *Introduction [and] Appendix*, vol. 2 of *The New Testament in the Original Greek* (London: Macmillan and Co., 1881), 251.

7. Westcott and Hort, *Introduction [and] Appendix*, 2–3.

8. Frederic Kenyon, *Our Bible and the Ancient Manuscripts*, rev. A. W. Adams (New York: Harper & Brothers, 1958), 55.

Chapter 12: The Text of the Old Testament

1. See Harry Minkoff, "The Aleppo Codex: Ancient Bible from the Ashes," *Bible Review* 7 (August 1991): 22–27, 38–40.

2. David Noel Freedman, Astrid B. Beck, Bruce E. Zuckerman, Marilyn J. Lundberg, and James A. Sanders, eds., *The Leningrad Codex: A Facsimile Edition* (Grand Rapids: Eerdmans, 1998). See also James A. Sanders and Astrid Beck, "The Leningrad Codex: Rediscovering the Oldest Complete Hebrew Bible," *Bible Review* (August 1997): 32–41, 46.

3. Cited by Frederic Kenyon, *Our Bible and the Ancient Manuscripts*, rev. A. W. Adams (New York: Harper & Brothers, 1958), 78–79.

4. On the Old Testament text, see B. J. Roberts, "The Old Testament Manuscripts, Text and Versions," in *The Cambridge History of the Bible*, vol. 2, ed. G. W. F. Lampe (Cambridge: Cambridge University Press, 1969), 1–26; also N. R. Lightfoot, "Canon and Text of the Old Testament," in *The World and Literature of the Old Testament*, ed. John T. Willis (Austin: Sweet, 1979), 41–70.

5. A replica is now on display instead of the original Isaiah Scroll (Isaiah A). See Hershel Shanks, "The Shrine of the Book—Where Nothing Has Changed," *Biblical Archaeology Review* 19 (September/October, 1993): 78–79.

6. The list is given by James C. VanderKam, *The Dead Sea Scrolls Today* (Grand Rapids: Eerdmans, 1994), 30–31.

7. The Qumran manuscripts are conveniently identified. The *Q* stands for Qumran, the number before the *Q* for the cave in which the manuscript was found, the abbreviation after the *Q* for the contents of the manuscript, the suspended letter for the number of the manuscript.

8. Roberts, "The Old Testament: Manuscripts, Text and Versions," in *The Cambridge History of the Bible*, vol. 2, 26.

9. J. Weingreen, *Introduction to the Critical Study of the Text of the Hebrew Bible* (Oxford: Clarendon, 1982), 96.

Chapter 13: Ancient Versions: The Old Testament

1. For a translation and introduction to the letter, see R. J. H. Shutt in *The Old Testament Pseudepigrapha*, vol. 2, ed. by James H. Charlesworth (Garden City, N.Y.: Doubleday, 1985), 7–34.

2. Nina Collins suggests a coregency of two years for Ptolemies I and II and that the translation was made after the death of Ptolemy I. Collins, "281 BCE: The Year of the Translation of the Pentateuch into Greek under Ptolemy II," in *Septuagint, Scrolls and Cognate Writings*, ed. George J. Brooks and Barnabas Lindars (Atlanta: Scholars, 1992), 412–14, 444–48. Collins goes on to say that, though problems remain, "the account of Aristeas concerning the translation of the Law is essentially true" (476).

3. Philo, *Life of Moses*, 2. 41.

4. See J. A. L. Lee, *A Lexical Study of the Septuagint Version of the Pentateuch*, ed. Harry M. Orlinsky (Chico, Calif.: Scholars, 1983), 146–47.

5. Adapting the words of A. D. Nock, "The Vocabulary of the New Testament," *Journal of Biblical Literature* 52 (1933): 138.

Chapter 14: The Canon of the Scriptures

1. See Roger Beckwith, *The Old Testament Canon of the New Testament Church and Its Background in Early Judaism* (Grand Rapids: Eerdmans, 1985), 115, 220–22.

2. See Jack P. Lewis, "What Do We Mean by Jabneh?" *The Journal of Bible and Religion* 32 (1964): 125–32; Beckwith, *The Old Testament Canon of the New Testament*

Church, 276–77; also N. R. Lightfoot, "Canon and Text of the Old Testament," in *The World and Literature of the Old Testament,* ed. John T. Willis (Austin: Sweet, 1979), 41–60.

3. Josephus, *Against Apion* 1. 8.

4. On the cessation of Jewish prophecy, see Beckwith, *The Old Testament Canon of the New Testament Church,* 369–76.

5. Cited by Eusebius, *Ecclesiastical History* 6. 25.

6. Justin Martyr, *First Apology* 67. 3.

7. See Everett Ferguson, "Canon Muratori; Date and Provenance," *Studia Patristica* 18 (1982): 677–83.

8. The two letters may refer to 2 and 3 John or to 1 and 2 John. Earlier the list identifies the Apostle John by quoting from 1 John, which raises the question whether the two letters exclude or include the previously cited letter of 1 John.

9. For an English translation of the Muratorian Fragment, see E. Hennecke, *New Testament Apocrypha,* vol. 1, ed. W. Schneemelcher, trans. R. McL. Wilson (Philadelphia: Westminster, 1963), 42–45. See also Bruce M. Metzger, *The Canon of the New Testament: Its Origin, Development, and Significance* (Oxford: Clarendon, 1987), 191–201, 304–7; also F. F. Bruce, *The Canon of Scripture* (Downer's Grove, Ill.: InterVarsity, 1988), 158–69.

10. Eusebius, *Ecclesiastical History* 6. 25. This, along with other third- and fourth-century documents on the canon, is conveniently assembled by Schneemelcher, *New Testament Apocrypha,* vol. 1, 52–60, and by Metzger, *The Canon of the New Testament,* 305–15.

11. According to Greek fragments of Origen's Catenae ("chains" of comments), cited by Schneemelcher, *New Testament Apocrypha,* vol. 1, 55.

12. A fuller quotation of the passage, with discussion, may be seen in Metzger, *The Canon of the New Testament,* 139.

13. Eusebius, *Ecclesiastical History* 3. 25. Eusebius is ambivalent on Revelation, first listing it with the acknowledged books, then including it with those that are rejected. It is "rejected by some, but others count it among the recognized books."

14. Athanasius, *Festal Epistle* 39.

Chapter 15: The Apocryphal Books

1. For additional information on the Apocrypha, see Bruce M. Metzger, *An Introduction to the Apocrypha* (New York: Oxford University Press, 1957); see especially Metzger's chapter, "A Brief History of the Apocrypha in the Christian Church," 175–204.

2. On Philo in particular, see the discussion by E. Earle Ellis, "The Old Testament Canon in the Early Church," in *Mikra: Text, Translation, Reading and Interpretation of the Hebrew Bible in Ancient Judaism and Early Christianity* (Minneapolis: Fortress, 1990), 657–58.

3. See Carey A. Moore, "Book of Judith," in D. N. Freedman et al., eds., *The Anchor Bible Dictionary,* vol. 3 (New York: Doubleday, 1992), 1119–22. But for other historical problems of Judith, see Metzger, *An Introduction to the Apocrypha,* 50–51.

4. Article VI of the Thirty-Nine Articles of Religion, issued in 1562. See Metzger's discussion, *An Introduction to the Apocrypha,* 190–92.

5. The Assumption of Moses and 1 Enoch are from what is known as the Old Testament Apocrypha or as the Old Testament Pseudepigrapha. See H. F. D. Sparks, ed., *The Apocryphal Old Testament* (Oxford: Clarendon, 1984) and James H. Charlesworth, ed., *The Old Testament Pseudepigrapha,* 2 vols. (New York: Doubleday, 1983).

6. See Roger Beckwith, *The Old Testament Canon of the New Testament Church* (Grand Rapids: Eerdmans, 1985), 396, 401–3.

7. The standard edition of these works is that of E. Hennecke, *New Testament Apocrypha*, 2 vols, ed. W. Schneemelcher, trans. R. McL. Wilson (Philadelphia: Westminster, 1963–65). See also Bruce M. Metzger's section on Apocryphal literature, *The Canon of the New Testament: Its Origin, Development, and Significance* (Oxford: Clarendon, 1987), 165–89.

Chapter 16: The English Bible to 1611

1. As quoted by Margaret Deanesly, *The Lollard Bible and Other Medieval Biblical Versions* (Cambridge: Cambridge University Press, 1920), 246. Deanesly's book is the standard work on the Bible during this period, but corrections have been suggested. See Anne Hudson, *Lollards and Their Books* (London: Hambledon, 1985), 105–10.

2. This statement, preserved in the sixteenth-century work of John Foxe, *Acts and Monuments,* is often quoted in biographies of Tyndale. For a recent biography and the quotation, see David Daniell, *William Tyndale: A Biography* (New Haven: Yale University Press, 1994), 79.

3. From Erasmus' 1516 edition of the Greek New Testament, in his *Paraclesis,* that is, his "Exhortation" to the reader.

4. "W. T. to the Reader" in *Tyndale's Old Testament, Being the Pentateuch of 1530, Joshua to 2 Chronicles of 1537, and Jonah. In a modern-spelling edition and with an introduction by David Daniell* (New Haven: Yale University Press, 1992), 5.

5. Daniell, *Tyndale,* 213.

6. But in John 3:16, 18, Tyndale translated "only son."

7. The words of Hugh Latimer to Nicholas Ridley at their martyrdom in Oxford, applied in a deeper sense to Tyndale by Frederic Kenyon, *Our Bible and the Ancient Manuscripts,* rev. A. W. Adams (New York: Harper & Brothers, 1958), 290.

8. J. F. Mozley argues that the Bible sent out among the people was the Coverdale Bible of 1535. Mozley, *Coverdale and His Bibles* (London: Lutterworth, 1953), 113–15.

9. On the background of the KJV, see William Barlow, *The Conference at Hampton Court, January 14, 1603* (reprint, Norwood, N.J.: W. J. Johnson, 1975); Gustavus S. Paine, *The Men Behind the King James Version* (reprint, Grand Rapids: Baker, 1977); Olga S. Opfell, *The King James Bible Translators* (Jefferson, N.C.: McFarland, 1982).

10. The KJV preface has been reprinted many times and is often available in books on the history of the English Bible and on the KJV. The American Bible Society has reprinted the preface in booklet form, ed. Erroll F. Rhodes and Liana Lupas (New York: American Bible Society, 1997).

11. The 1613 edition is often dated 1613, 11. It is thought that much of it was printed in 1611 but was not published until 1613. But the whole question is surrounded with uncertainties. See Alfred W. Pollard, *Records of the English Bible* (London: Oxford University Press, 1911), 66–73.

Chapter 17: Recent Translations of the English Bible

1. See Bruce M. Metzger, Robert C. Dentan, and Walter Harrelson, *The Making of the New Revised Standard Version of the Bible* (Grand Rapids: Eerdmans, 1991), 60–61.

2. See Ibid., 5–8, 57.

3. The NRSV footnote reads, "Gk [Greek] *the husband of one wife.*"

4. On the many English translations, see Bruce M. Metzger, *The Bible in Translation: Ancient and English Versions* (Grand Rapids: Baker, 2001), 55–290; also Jack P. Lewis, *The English Bible from KJV to NIV: A History and Evaluation,* 2d ed. (Grand Rapids: Baker, 1991).

5. See N. R. Lightfoot, "Two Recent Translations: A Study in Translation Principle," *Restoration Quarterly* 11 (1968): 89–100.

6. For a rather severe critique of the style of the New International Version, see Barclay M. Newman Jr., "Readability and the New International Version of the New Testament," *The Bible Translator* 31 (1980): 325–36.

Chapter 18: "My Words Will Not Pass Away"

1. Frederic Kenyon, *Our Bible and the Ancient Manuscripts,* rev. A. W. Adams (New York: Harper & Brothers, 1958), 55.

Index

Index

Neil R. Lightfoot (Ph.D., Duke University) serves as Frank Pack Distinguished Professor of New Testament at Abilene Christian University in Abilene, Texas. He is the author of several books, including *Everyone's Guide to Hebrews.*